Why study creativity?

Reflections & Lessons from the International Center for Studies in Creativity

Why study
creativity?

Reflections & Lessons from the
International Center for Studies in Creativity

Edited by Jon Michael Fox & Ronni Lea Fox

ICSC Press
International Center for Studies in Creativity
Buffalo State, State University of New York
Buffalo, NY, U.S.A.

ICSC PRESS
INTERNATIONAL CENTER *for*
STUDIES *in* CREATIVITY
BUFFALO STATE · The State University of New York

ICSC Press
International Center for Studies in Creativity
SUNY Buffalo State
1300 Elmwood Avenue
Buffalo, NY 14222, USA
icscpress.com

ISBN: 978-0-9849795-6-1

Library of Congress Control Number: 2016940546

Simultaneously published in multiple formats, both print and electronic.
For alternative versions and to discover other titles, visit icscpress.com.

Managing Editor: Paul Reali
Graduate Assistant Editor: Molly Holinger
Book Design: Kevin D. Opp
Cover Image: DrAfter123, licensed from iStockphoto

This book is dedicated to all of you who wish for the creativity you packed away in the 4th grade. Yet, be careful what you wish for. When you get your creativity back, there is no *going* back. You can't cross a chasm in two small leaps.

Contents

Part 3: Business & Organizational Creativity

Part 4: Creativity in Education

Part 5: Applications of Creativity

Introduction: An Orientation to the Study of Creativity

Jon Michael Fox and Ronni Lea Fox

What's in it for me? This is the question we all ask when faced with change. Implicitly or explicitly, we ask this question, or its variants, when we are faced with accepting a new paradigm, taking a risk, letting our curiosity lead to action, or any other event that happens in our daily lives.

We are frequently asked, "What do I do with a degree in creativity?" This question is a variant of "What's in it for me?" This book contains stories of actual applications of creativity, creative problem solving, and change leadership, told by those who studied at SUNY Buffalo State's International Center for Studies in Creativity. We hope that you will find a chapter that resonates with you and answers for you the value of studying creativity, the value in applying creativity in personal reflection, for the potential for personal growth, or for reducing the fear of change.

The "What's in it for me?" question is simple. The answer, not so much. Read on. Perhaps you will identify with one of the chapters.

What is Creativity Anyway?

There is no universal definition of creativity. In fact, there are at least 365 definitions, one for each day of the year. (Don't ask how we know. Suffice it to say that as we went through the process of gathering the data it stopped being fun along about September.) Not only is creativity trans-disciplinary, it crosses *all* disciplines. It is a set of thinking skills, behavioral skills, and affective skills that can be applied wherever creativity is required.

Not everything requires creativity. For example, when manufacturing widgets, widget number one and widget number 1,000 ought to be the same. No creativity required. None wanted. But when you want an outcome that is both new and useful *at the same time,* creativity is the stuff of it. We have some catchy couplets for describing creativity: novel and useful, new and useful, novel and appropriate, original and adaptable to reality. Describe it the way you want, but the couplet remains. The outcome has to have both qualities: some level of newness and some level of usefulness. The degree of each is up to the individual.

In addition to *new and useful,* here are some other ways to consider creativity.

> Creativity is an essential life skill. It is a way of turning challenges into opportunities, seeing new solutions to old problems, seeing old problems in new ways and anticipating the future. We all have the capacity to think creatively, and in various ways we are called on to use our creative problem-solving skills (Puccio & Murdock, 2001).

> Creativity is the product of novel and appropriate solutions to open-ended problems in any domain of human activity (Amabile, 1996).

> Creativity is the generation of novel and useful ideas (Gryskiewicz, 1987).

> Creativity is the ability to modify self-imposed constraints (Ackoff & Vergara, 1981).

> Creativity is an arbitrary harmony, an unexpected astonishment, a habitual revelation, a familiar surprise, a generous selfishness, a vital triviality, a disciplined freedom, an intoxicating steadiness, a repeated initiation, a predictable gamble, an ephemeral solidity, a unifying difference, a demanding satisfier, a miraculous expectation, an accustomed amazement (Prince, 1969).

> When you are able to think in a way that is completely out of the norm, process information in a manner that is out of the ordinary, and when you can find multiple solutions to different situations and problems, then you are a creative person (Julio G. Urrutia, Creative Studies minor student, SUNY Buffalo State, personal conversation).

> It is important to note that innovation is not the same as creativity: innovation is the successful implementation of creative ideas by an organization (Amabile, 1995).

Dr. Ruth Noller, an early pioneer in the field (and a mathematician) presented it as a simple yet elegant equation: Creativity equals the function of *attitude* multiplied by *knowledge, imagination,* and *evaluation.* The formula is illustrative in that it gives us a way of thinking about how creativity works.

$$C = fa(KIE)$$

Where:

C—the "size" of creativity
f—a symbol for the "function of"
a—attitude (the driver of creativity)
K—knowledge
I—imagination
E—evaluation

The size of C—just how much creativity is being displayed—depends on the items on the right side of the equation. We commonly ascribe imagination to children. The alternative assumptions are that adults, with a positive, engaging attitude, are strong in knowledge and evaluation skills but less so in imagination. Causes are many but suffice it to say, imagination is reinforced in children but less so in adults. Albert Einstein was quoted as saying, "Imagination is more important than knowledge." Yet there is evidence that adults do not get regular reinforcement for being imaginative. Unfortunately, the result is that displayed creativity is reduced.

Myths of Creativity

The myths of creativity abound. The myths are reinforced by society in general and supported by the media. You are *born with it* or you're not. Creativity is so *mysterious* that it is not knowable. Creativity is *magic*. Creativity has the quality of *madness*. You have to be *crazy* to be creative. Creativity comes from *outside* the person. It is from the *muse*—question the muse and you'll chase it away.

We have a technical term for the myths: they're crap. Creativity is very demo-cratic. Everybody has some. When you joined the human race you got a share. Unfortunately, many of us packed our creativity away in about the 4th grade. This phenomenon is so pervasive, we call it the 4th grade slump. Here is the reality: creativity is a teachable and learnable skill, just like reading and writing. You *can* get your creativity back at any time.

Headline-making creativity is just that: headlines. It is decidedly not common. The really good stuff is *everyday* creativity—so common we tend to overlook it. Everyday creativity is making a really good soup, solving a thorny problem at work, daydreaming, letting your curiosity drive your day.

A Basic Schema: 4Ps of Creativity

When dissecting creativity to understand what it is and how it works, we chunk it up into four pieces: the nature of the creative Person, the Processes the creative person uses to generate a creative outcome, or Product, and the Press (those things pressing in on us that help or hinder our creativity). For convenience we call this the 4Ps: Person, Process, Product, and Press (Rhodes, 1961). Separating the 4Ps for the sake of study and understanding is not the same as creativity itself. The four areas work together all the time. In the scientific inquiry into creativity there is another technical term for this interaction: it's a mess. Messy or not, it's time to set aside the myths of creativity. We know a lot about creativity. Focused research about creativity has been going on for well over 60 years. Research opens new questions. To paraphrase Einstein, if we knew all the answers we wouldn't call it research, would we?

ABCs of Creativity

What might you expect to get for your trade if you study creativity? A handy way to think about this is the ABCs of creativity: *Affective* creativity, *Behavioral* creativity, and *Cognitive* creativity. One might say that when learning the new skill sets we start with the cognitive and work backwards to the affective. Although that is not exactly true, it helps in understanding what happens from a practical and reflective point of view.

Cognitive Creativity

This is where we start. Cognitive creativity can be thought of in three elements of thinking: rational, cognitive, and semantic. Rational is logical and repeatable. Cognitive is a thinking skill set. Semantic is language-based (after all, language *is* the currency of human beings). The typical and probably most well-known cognitive tool is Brainstorming. (A cook gets a spatula and a pan and a carpenter gets a hammer and a saw; if you want to be creative, you ought to get something.) There are hundreds of rational, cognitive, semantic tools for generating options and for selecting options.

I came across a story about the effect of semantics. A blind beggar had a sign beside his cup of pencils. The sign read "I'm blind. Please help." Few passersby stopped to donate money. He then had a new sign made. It read, "It's a beautiful day and I can't see it." The second sign worked well. Semantics matter.

Cognitive creativity is an easy and appropriate place to start when you want to get your creativity back.

Behavioral Creativity

Behavioral creativity seems to happen as our thinking changes. Our thinking changes our behavior. We overtly use affirmative judgment and stay open minded. We tend to collect data before making a decision. Creative people eschew what the politicians are famous for: *data-free* analysis.

Affective Creativity

This is who you are. It is the gold standard of creativity. Affective creativity is self-actualization. Words like daydreaming, curiosity, playfulness, humor, and tolerance of ambiguity come to mind. Study creativity and this will happen to you. You get the creativity back that you packed away in the 4th grade. Caution: remember the adage, "Be careful what you wish for." If you study creativity you will become different. When you get your creativity back there is no *going* back.

Is the Degree in Creativity Worth It?

Good question. We value what we measure. Typical metrics for a college degree are gainful employment, salaries, and alumni satisfaction rates. Yet these metrics fall short of explaining why college is worth it. What if you were to reframe the question, "Is your well-being worth it?" The degree in creativity is a stepping-stone to getting your creativity back. The real benefit is a life that matters.

The following narrative from Busteed's (2013) article in the *Gallup Business Journal* makes this clear:

> *What should be the ultimate outcome of a college education?* When I first joined Gallup about a year ago, I spent six months informally asking college presidents and trustees this very question. After dozens of interviews, a pattern emerged. Although the words and perspectives differed, the answers were consistent: "To improve one's lot in life" or "To prepare people for long-term success in life." Those are solid, inspiring answers. So I asked the next obvious question: "How are you measuring this?" The unanimous answer was: "We aren't."
>
> There is an expression: "We value what we measure." It seems clear that leaders in higher education are not measuring what they value right now. But there is an alternative—one that would lead to better educational and career outcomes for students and provide an affirmative answer to the question of whether college is worth the time, money, and effort.
>
> Most people would agree that helping someone attain a better, fuller life is much more important than good grades and a degree. These same people also stress that college prepares a person not just for a first job out of college but for many different jobs over his or her lifetime. But how do you measure these longer-term outcomes? Gallup has conducted research that can point higher education in the right direction.
>
> *Well-being closely tied to education.* [Gallup has] discovered what the most satisfied and successful people do and, subsequently, why they rate their lives highly. In other words, we are studying the well-being of people around the world. Our research reinforces the fact that the

ultimate outcome of an education is fundamentally about well-being. People often view well-being as happiness or wealth, but it is much more than that, and it is closely tied to education.

From our data, Gallup found five essential elements of well-being: Career, Social, Financial, Physical, and Community. These well-being elements represent the broad categories that are essential for most people to live a life that matters.

- Career well-being: how you occupy your time—or simply liking what you do every day.

- Social well-being: having strong relationships and love in your life.

- Financial well-being: effectively managing your economic life.

- Physical well-being: having good health and enough energy to get things done on a daily basis.

- Community well-being: the sense of engagement you have with the area where you live.

Of those five elements, Gallup finds that career well-being is the most important predictor of well-being across the board. (para. 5-15)

These elements of well-being are also the earmarks of self actualization, and self-actualization and creativity, Maslow (1976) pointed out, may in fact be the same thing.

Creative and Critical Thinking: Essential Life Skills

We give much credence to critical thinking, and justifiably so. It addresses the question of what to think about any content knowledge—a useful and necessary skill—highly prized for the continuation of the species. When you go to a surgeon, you want him to know exactly what to think. Alternatively, creative thinking works across the board. Creative thinking adds "process skills" to any content area. Dr. Aaron Podolefsky, then-President of Buffalo State, noted, "Critical thinking should be used only in service to creative thinking" (personal conversation, May 2, 2011).

Both critical thinking and creative thinking are necessary. When faced with a challenge you will have to make a decision: is there a workable policy or formula already in place, or will you have to invent something new that is appropriate to the challenge?

IBM Corporation (2010) surveyed 1,500 CEOs and found creative thinking skills are a top need:

Increasingly interconnected economies, enterprises, societies and governments have given rise to vast new opportunities. But a surprising number of CEOs told us they feel ill-prepared for today's more complex environment.

With few exceptions, CEOs expect continued disruption in one form or another. The new economic environment, they agree, is substantially more volatile, much more uncertain, increasingly complex and structurally different. An Industrial Products CEO in the Netherlands summed up the sentiments of many when he described last year as "a wake-up call," adding that "it felt like looking into the dark with no light at the end of the tunnel." (p. 14)

Competition, complexity, and change require responses to problems and opportunities that we haven't even seen yet. Businesses are demanding creative thinking skills in their new hires. Be ready to participate.

Useful Things to Contemplate

We are all Swiss cheese. We all have holes—areas for development. Maybe we want to fill them in, maybe we don't. Interested in finding out what your Swiss cheese looks like? Here is a writing exercise for you:

1. This is where I am...

2. This is where I want to be...

   - What are my goals?

   - What do I want to change?

   - What do I wish for?

3. This is my "path"...

Summary

There you have it. Everybody is Swiss cheese. Because you are the locus of creativity, your creativity will be different than mine. Push back on the myths and find that creativity is knowable, learnable and part of being healthy. The 4Ps of creativity are a convenient way of organizing the inquiry into creativity, yet know that they are inextricably connected. Affective skills, behavioral skills, and cognitive skills are just that: they are teachable, learnable skills. No magic, just hard work. For your life-long well-being, unpack the creativity that you stored away in the 4th grade. Is studying creativity worth it? The contributors of the articles that follow say yes.

References

Ackoff, R. L. & Vergara, E. (1981). Creativity in problem solving and planning: A review. *European Journal of Operational Research, 7,* 1-13.

Amabile, T. M. (1995). Discovering the unknowable, managing the unmanageable. In C. M. Ford & D. A. Gioia (Eds.), *Creative action in organizations.* Newbury Park, CA: Sage.

Amabile, T. M. (1996). *Creativity in context: Update to the social psychology of creativity.* Boulder, CO: Westview Press.

Busteed, B. (August 27, 2013). Is college worth it? *Gallup Business Journal.* Retrieved from http://www.gallup.com/businessjournal/164108/college-worth. aspx

Gryskiewicz, S. (1987). Predictable creativity. In S. G. Isaksen (Ed.), *Frontiers of creativity research: Beyond the basics* (pp. 305-313). Buffalo, NY: Bearly Limited.

IBM Corporation (2010). *Capitalizing on complexity: Insights from the global chief executive officer study.* Somers, NY: IBM Global Business Services.

Maslow, A. H. (1976). The farther reaches of human nature. New York, NY: Penguin. (Original work published 1971)

Prince, G. M. (1969). *The practice of creativity.* Cambridge, MA: Synectics.

Puccio, G. J. & Murdock, M. C. (2001). Creative thinking: An essential life skill. In A. Costa (Ed.), *Developing minds: A sourcebook for teaching thinking* (pp. 67-71). Alexandria, VA: ASCD.

Rhodes, M. (1961). An analysis of creativity. *Phi Beta Kappan, 42,* 305-310.

Part 1:
Personal Growth &
Transformation

Foraging and Cultivating: Creativity and the Nourishing of the Mind

Amy Frazier

The practice of relating to creativity in a deliberate fashion has allowed me to see into the world in a different way. The study of creativity sharpened my vision for the terrain around me, helping me learn to identify various products of the mind, including ideas that sprout from new thinking. This has had a tremendous impact on my life. It's not unlike the revolution in awareness we achieve when, to invoke a metaphor, we forgo the optimization and convenience of the grocery store as supplier of all of our nourishment and "return to the land" to feed our creative selves.

In fact, having a working understanding of creativity and the creative process is rather like knowing how to identify the right herbs and roots and berries to harvest in the wild, and how to best handle them to guard their potency. If we'd all had wise people leading us through the forest from an early age, teaching us how creativity appears in its various niches and stages of growth, then perhaps we wouldn't have need of the study. But we didn't. We were raised, many of us, in the industrialized farming of the mind, where standardized answers, like standardized testing, and standardized cultivars, were prized more highly than rough variance.

I don't mean to suggest we completely abandoned the wild side of our thinking. Of course we've continued to have strange ideas drift in on the wind; and of course we've often gone deliberately foraging for them on our own, tramping through the woods and undergrowth on the edge of town, at the frontier of the familiar. There are even some among us who seem to live comfortably in these more diversified and often thornier environments of the mind: highly creative thinkers who emerge from the forest on a regular basis, their baskets loaded with unusual discoveries. Instinctively, we understand that this dogged and curious search for new thinking feeds our minds in important ways. Taking chances, following hunches, embracing uncertainty. These are healthy creative practices.

On the other hand: I planted herbs and vegetables this summer, in two wooden planter boxes vacated by a neighbor. I purchased a few seed packets but mainly acquired the more dependable and identifiable plant starts. I released the starts from their small plastic boxes, and laid them in neat rows inside the planters. I tucked plastic name tags next to them, in case I should at some point lose the difference between oregano and thyme. No foraging here. Nothing "outside the box." Small boxes, in fact, transplanted into slightly larger ones. And all very cultivated, planned. As I considered the contradiction inherent in my none-too-wild planter boxes, I realized that while the importance of being able to identify creativity in the wild—and especially the courage to go tramping through the underbrush in the first place—can't be over-emphasized, there are some down-sides. It takes more energy and effort. There's a higher degree of uncertainty. Other people might be suspicious of your spikey, odd-featured discovery. You could go hungry. You could poison yourself.

So, to be honest, we don't always need to be foraging for the wild creative. We can cultivate it as well. In fact, we can be as deliberate about our creativity as we are about our gardens. This was one of the biggest discoveries for me about the study of creativity: I didn't always have to muck about in the underbrush for a new idea. I could design my thinking around the stages of the creative process, much as I designed my planter boxes. I could learn to depend upon the yield, and even, occasionally, the timing of the harvest.

To be successful with our creativity then, we need to both forage and cultivate. One looks to the wilder niches, and asks greater tolerance for uncertainty and unforeseen variety; the other depends upon steady tending of the environment and the ability to manage a yield over time.

Now, to extend the agricultural analogy, probably the worst thing we can do for the creative feeding of our minds is to come to depend exclusively upon the mental equivalent of the supermarket, where pyramids of gleaming ideas offer an image of abundance in what is really, upon closer inspection, a proliferation of standardization. Here, not only is there scant surprise or variance (i.e., novelty), but the sheer quantity and convenience lull us into believing that the mere act of choosing from what has been presented to us is sufficient exercise of our creative thinking. It's not. We've neither discovered the ideas, nor grown them on our own. Over time, the absence of those activities—discovering and growing—permits our creativity to atrophy. We become more consumers than creators, and ultimately less fit to creatively survive on the merits of our own thinking.

The study of creativity has permitted me to help people—myself included—determine when to go to the extra effort of foraging for new ideas or setting out to cultivate them. I'm able to demonstrate that acquiring all one's ideas at the market, no matter how attractively they're presented, is not the same thing as becoming a well-rounded creative thinker. And in a manner that serves my desire to serve the world, I'm becoming better able to see others' creative potential—both their promising wildernesses, and their planter boxes waiting to be filled. I'm learning how to support them accordingly, by accompanying them into the underbrush to forage, or by guiding them through a process of planful creative cultivation.

And here's why this matters so much, why it's so vitally important in our times: entering into the unknown in search of sustenance puts us in touch with our deepest nature; planning the garden helps to exercise the cleverness of our species' powerful, future-focused minds. Anytime we can reinforce these givens, we help to perpetuate our human creative endowment. In the face of that glorious opportunity, however, we live in a world where convenience and homogeneity rule. We are easily distracted by that which we're told we ought to desire; and in stuffing ourselves with those things which do not truly satisfy, we go hungry. Cheap calories and prefabricated ideas are equally debilitating.

But when we resist the easy abundance of standardized thinking and permit ourselves the work of foraging for ideas; and when we dedicate ourselves to the cultivation of varieties of thought across the span from seed to harvest, we nourish our minds. We feed ourselves with both the fruit of our creative thinking, and the satisfaction found in fully participating in the process. What I've observed in this, for myself and my clients, has been not only the excitement of watching an idea seed grow through its own proper stages, or the triumph found in daring to gnaw upon an idea root until it yields its own proper sweetness, but a deep investment in both process and outcome. It only makes sense: something we grow or discover leads us into dialogue with ourselves as we ascertain and elaborate its value; in so doing it becomes a part of us. Ideas are thus more firmly rooted, and our inquisitive minds ultimately better fed. My experience has taught me this: studying creativity enhances the skillfulness with which we are able to explore and tend to the wild spaces and gardens in our minds.

I Lead a Creative Life

Maisha Drayton

When I first entered the Creative Studies graduate program at SUNY Buffalo State, I had very specific expectations. I thought I would graduate and become a Creative Problem Solving facilitator and consultant, go on to pursue my doctorate, or at least simply apply what I learned to my then-position as a director in the non-profit sector.

Today, three years after I graduated, things are very different. The program exceeded all prior expectations, and I became a living, breathing product of the program.

I am a better parent, wife, friend, manager, and employee because of what I learned as a student of creativity. In creativity, we talk about the "4Ps" by which one can view creativity: Person, Processes, Products, and Press (environmental pressures and conditions). Believe it or not, the 4Ps of creativity apply to just about everything in life. In life there are people, processes, products, and presses. Once I figured out how to understand, navigate, communicate, and affect them creatively, everything fell into place. And when I learned the "lingo," including *trial and learn, deferring judgment,* and *in what ways might I...,* there was nothing stopping me from implementing creativity into my everyday thought process and way of speaking.

Being a textbook extrovert, I could go on and on about what I've learned and how I have benefited. However, I'll just end with this: "To live a creative life, we must lose our fear of being wrong" (Joseph Chilton Pearce). I lead a creative life, and it is thanks to my time at the ICSC.

Creativity: The Ultimate Challenge

Tiana Thompson

When I first began graduate school at SUNY Buffalo State, it was during a difficult period in my life. Prior to entering into the Creative Studies program I lost both of my grandparents a year apart. Because of their wisdom, guidance, and encouragement, their spirits gave me the courage to apply to graduate school. When I entered into the program I was unaware of what to expect. I walked in reserved, introverted, and unsure about my future. I knew at the time I was searching for something but didn't know quite what it was.

During the very first day of attending Creative Studies classes I felt at home. It was then that I realized that my classmates were all searching to find their way in the world just like me. I was able to observe and relate to them during my time as a graduate student. As I continued my studies in the program, I became more intrigued with the idea that I was finally learning how to be "content" with myself. I learned along the way that it's okay to make mistakes, to take risks, and to finally let my voice be heard. The program has given me the courage to be open to change, to challenge myself, and to be comfortable in my own skin.

Since graduating in May of 2013, I have prepared myself to use the tools from the Creative Studies program and to implement them in my career endeavors. I have published a book titled *Visually Paired Through Creativity*, which contains my artwork paired with the affective skills of Creative Problem Solving, exploring the parallels of creative thinking and art-making.

Affective skills in CPS enhance and balance the cognitive skills, and this influences the art-making process. Because art can be a therapeutic process, affective skills can be experimented with throughout, in the process from initial thought to incorporating them into the art-making process. Affective skills, I believe, are the driving force to creativity and provide a resource to positive change. Emotions set the foundation for creative ideas and concepts. My main objective as an artist is to visually interpret emotions to showcase in the art form. The reward is self-gratifying if affective skills are used properly.

For the past 10 years I have been working with students with developmental disabilities. My goal for the future is to create a series of interactive sensory books especially designed for these children. I would like to combine my love for children and my fascination with art to pursue a career as an art therapist. I think it is essential to instill creativity in everyone, especially children. My other career aspirations include branding my artwork into a variety of outlets including T-shirts, social media networking, and a series of books related to creativity in the arts.

Creativity challenges our strengths, weaknesses, thinking patterns, and creative potential. Without creativity we are all limited in changing the future. Creativity is the ultimate challenge that I love in life. It leads to unexpected wonder and excitement as I continue my career aspirations. I believe that my true passion and purpose in this world is to share my creativity with others. And so I say to the reader: embrace creativity.

What Studying Creativity Does to You

Doug Stevenson

Many people come to the International Center for Studies in Creativity at SUNY Buffalo State in mid-life or mid-career. They come because of a passion for creativity, and many because they seek greater alignment with creative pursuits in their lives. They come to acquire insights and skills that will enhance their position within their current jobs and help them get ahead, or to leapfrog to another life and career altogether.

When you make the commitment to study creativity, you make a commitment to change—because studying creativity will change you. And because they are changed, most students find it begins to change everything around them, also.

It is mostly wonderful and serendipitous. "Following your bliss" is an awesome experience. But it also can be disruptive, like innovation can be. And one form of innovation is personal "re-creation."

Like Joseph Campbell's paradigmatic protagonist, you will have embarked on a "hero's journey," which means descending into a bit of darkness before you get to the light. There will be many new heights, but also some new depths. The good news is that you will have newly acquired Creative Problem Solving skills to help you make your choices and guide your way in handling your new successes and the challenges they bring.

Since graduation, I have worked with many organizations and companies on a variety of challenges, including new product ideation, change management, team building, process improvement, branding, and more. I have spent a fair share of that time working with Fortune 500 companies—and there is clearly a need for creative thinking and opportunity there. However, in recent years, I have shifted my focus to non-profits. My clients have included children's theatres, arts centers, prisoner rehabilitation programs, cultural exchanges, campaigns for human afflictions, and homeless shelters.

It is challenging, stimulating, creative, and game-changing work. True to Gandhi's admonition to "be the change you wish to see in the world," the work is aligned with my values, as well as my interest in creativity. My studies made this work possible.

Now my life is *all* about creativity. That was my vow, my mission, my goal, even before I embarked on my Master of Science in Creativity; now I can say that is fully true.

I find that creativity has changed the way I live my life in general, around things big and little—how I handle communication with colleagues, friends and family; how I make purchase decisions; or even how I fix a broken shoelace or screw in a light bulb.

So, not all of what I do has profound significance for the world, but all that I do has been profoundly changed.

Creativity studies has made me a more engaged, more connected, and more powerful agent for positive change in the world, and ultimately, more alive. It assists me in all the little things. Life is but a series of moments strung together, and for me creative thinking permeates every one of those moments. Creativity is, after all, the ubiquitous, primal force in the universe. Studying creativity helped me to understand that, and to harness it.

What Learning Creativity Has Done for My Life

Dixie Hudson

When asked what I do, I usually say I am an interior designer and educator. However, what I truly am is a life-long learner. I am keen to take on adventures, travel to explore different cultures, and to learn about new ideas. I enjoy attending conferences and listening to keynote speakers who often tell of their latest passions and commitments. (At one time I wouldn't have said that these were characteristics of creative people—but I would eventually find that out.)

Following this vein, I had the opportunity to return to school and had been looking for just the right Master's degree program for a couple of years. But what did I want to focus on? I looked into advanced lighting programs and sustainability programs, either of which would relate to my teaching career. Yet there was something missing; neither area provided a very different perspective from what I was already doing. I kept searching for an "interesting" program.

In my search I stumbled upon the International Center for Studies in Creativity at SUNY Buffalo State, and was fascinated by the idea of digging deeper into the topic of creativity. Creativity was a topic that I hadn't studied directly, and I felt I wanted to learn more. I read the course descriptions and seriously felt that this program was written for me. It captured me in a way that no other program had.

With strengths as an ideator and implementer (as the FourSight profile would later show me), I dove into the exploration of creativity and was jolted alive. *What is creativity? How does it affect our lives? Why do we need to study it?* I thought that I *was* creative, because as an interior designer I participated in a creative field. I thought that some people were just naturally creative. To learn instead that everyone is creative (or, has creative potential), that creativity can be enhanced, and that there is a creative process to work with, gave me new ways to understand my students and myself. Since there has been more than 60 years of research into the topic of creativity, I had a major adventure of exploration ahead of me.

I have had the honor to be taught by the most amazing professors, who have demonstrated their creativity through living its principles. They have brought to the classroom techniques that have truly sparked a desire and curiosity in me to know more. The environment quickly became one of trust, and my cohort synthesized into a supportive group with a huge array of knowledge and differing perspectives from many disciplines. This experience gave me a gift of insight into how I teach my own classes, with more focus on creating an environment to develop creativity and curiosity in my students, and to bring back the joy of learning.

How might one describe to others an environment that has the power to transform the way we approach life? I have personally witnessed changes in people. The study of creativity introduced such a different way to approach challenges and each other. It was a process and understanding that developed into so much more meaning, that to those involved was transformative.

The process allows one to dig deeper and drill to the core of a challenge—one that will offer meaning and understanding greater than we imagined. Was I—and are you—really looking for such an insightful, valuable challenge?

Once one has witnessed the strength of creativity to develop a deeper understanding of challenges, and a more playful approach to solving them, one cannot turn back. It infuses into one's life a delightful, unexpected awareness of the creativity that is in us all, and a confidence to live life with a vision of what is possible. The process is an abstract yet tangible narrative with infinite possibilities.

Creative Studies Courses Changed My GPA... and My Outlook

Ryan Irish

I can honestly say I apply what I have learned in Creative Studies courses at SUNY Buffalo State to almost every class I am in. It has changed not just my GPA but also my outlook on school.

The course that best represents my use of what I learned in Creative Studies outside of a Creative Studies class was Creative Poetry Writing. For some time I have wished to use my creative writing abilities to produce rhyming-literature books for children that would help them learn to read while educating them about an important topic at the same time. While taking Introduction to Creative Studies, I began to work on several books dealing with a range of topics, such as AIDS, depression, and politics. In Creative Poetry Writing, I then took these books even further in their content and message.

Applying what I had learned in Creative Studies with Creative Poetry Writing was a success for me. First of all, instead of just starting a story and working with something that came off the top of my head, I began to break down potential topics using the idea-generating tool Brainstorming. For instance, if faced with a choice between writing a political story or a story about autism, I would ask, "In what ways is a children's story about autism better then a story about politics?" After diverging and converging, I determined that a political story is irrelevant to children. They can't vote, they thought President Bush is a great guy because "he's always smiling," yet autism is something absolutely relevant. Most children see autistic kids in their daily lives—they just don't know it. It's just a strange kid to them, and they don't know why kids with autism act the way they do.

I try to give myself about 30 minutes to write down as many ideas for the story as possible. Some are crazy, like having a child learn about autism by fighting a bully. Other story lines are rational and tangible, such as having a nightmare or acting strangely and not knowing why. In story writing, I now try to take into account a notion I never would have before: *there is no wrong answer.* Crazy ideas create real potential. I might not use the crazy idea, but the crazy idea can lead to one I can use. And, it's great for my mind to get off-task just for a second and laugh—a moment of incubation that actually helps the creative mind work better. Next, I sit down and put check marks down next to the ideas I like and try to formulate a story from this standpoint. Alternatively, I might choose the five ideas I like *least* and try to make a story from them, which, suprisingingly, produces some interesting results.

In writing creative poetry I use many of the tools I learned in my Creative Studies courses. The one I use most frequently is called Word Dance. When rhyming, Word Dance is a must. I like to sit around with one word and try to make as many rhymes with it as I can. I use the tool Highlighting to select the words I like the best. Another really useful tool is Clustering, where similar ideas are placed together. I can think up amazing stories that I had no intention of writing, when clustering.

I was Brainwriting once when I started off on a tangent about "what if fish were instruments?" I ended up diverging even more—for a story I was writing about politics—to produce a children's book about the Sea of Sound. It is a book about instruments hiding deep below the sea as evil corporations try to steal their notes. It's foolish, but it shows how ridiculously well the creative process works. It allows me to relax my mind while at the same time pushing it to work.

I apply what I have learned in Creative Studies to almost every class I am in. It has changed my GPA and my outlook on school. Instead of rushing through things for the quickest option, I now sort through options to find the most efficient and effective. By taking time to use a process, I help myself to learn better, and to be a better thinker and a better student.

My Journey Through My Studies

Randah Taher

E ven before I completed the Master of Science in Creativity and Change Leadership from SUNY Buffalo State, I was able to put it to work.

My experience at the International Center for Studies in Creativity was a springboard for all great things destined to happen. The people, the classes, and the order in which courses were taken, whether intentionally or not, were key ingredients for the life I was baking. It all started when I first met my "Lucky 7" cohort in 2007 and learned about being a facilitator of Creative Problem Solving. While not far from the training field, I had assumed the position of being an expert in the topic rather than the process; CPS works the other way, where facilitators focus on process over content.

Creativity icons like E. Paul Torrence shaped the way I look at expertise and manifest it almost invisibly as a facilitator. I started searching for my own heroes and legends and found many examples that enriched my view of the world. I suddenly found myself comfortable as a minority of one (Torrance, 2006) when I decided to become a generalist rather than a specialist. I have trained and consulted in creative thinking, teams, and environments, and while still studying, started creating idea clinics where I help people come up with ideas to solve their small and big problems using some of the divergent and convergent tools learned.

The process of playing with ideas before translating them into action plans came directly from a discovery I made while learning the FourSight assessment tool, in which my score showed a clear preference for Ideation and Implementation (foursightonline.com). This tool was an eye-opener for me, and changed how I see the people I work and live with. It made sense to focus on what I am really good at and expand it to the idea generation and realization workshops I later conducted. FourSight and other assessments we took revealed more hidden—and not so hidden—secrets that reside within and around us. Things like KEYS

(Amabile, 1996) or Ekvall's 10 Dimensions of Creative Environments (Lauer, 1994), opened further doors to my organizational exploration. While designing some of my assignments, I was able to build a bigger picture by connecting Ekvall's 10 Dimensions to the Islamic Golden Age, a creative era in history (Taher, 2008b), and then take it a step further to learn more about how the space we live in affects our own creativity.

This in itself took me through another path of its own.

Creative Spaces

Learning about creative spaces was greatly motivating. Not only how we can change the surroundings to reach more aspects of our own creativity, but also how the environment can affect our own thinking. Concepts such as the effect of ceiling heights (Meyers-Levy & Zho, 2007), the availability of natural material, or how the memories associated with a place can make us think more expansively—these were of immense importance in how I took this learning further (Taher, 2008c).

The 2nd Creativity and Innovation Management Conference, which I participated in during my third semester in 2008, was a starting point in the direction of organizational creativity through space design. I later used this skill in consulting in creative space design, be it an individual experimentation room or an international incubation center for entrepreneurs such as the Impact Hub Dubai (impacthub.ae).

Creative Development

The crowning of my studies came in the shape of my Master's Project, the program's capstone creation. At the time, I was also working at United Way Toronto (unitedwaytoronto.com), and was given one main goal: put together a leadership program for young people working in the nonprofit sector, one like no other program before.

A straightforward but not simple task, I immediately reassembled my brain to think of it in a completely different way.

The process was unique, as the program development stage took six weeks instead of the allocated 12, using design charrette-style facilitation. The choices for modules given to participants were built based on grounds-up planning instead of the usual top-to-bottom cascading decisions. The learning was immediately applied in a community-based project, involving even more people in the success of the program. Finally, the network of resource providers grew organically as the number of organizations who wanted to be involved outgrew the number of spots available. This by itself led to increased funding (three times more before the program had even launched), extending the reach to more participants, and eventually extending the program's life span to several more years. Fortunately, while building the Creative Institute for Toronto's Young Leaders (CITY Leaders) for United Way Toronto, I was documenting the process of putting it together, and was able to submit it as my Master's Project (Taher, 2008a).

Like I said, I had to reassemble my brain to get it right.

Creative Career Changes

Perhaps the biggest leap I made from the design-and-build part of my studies was accepting a position as a lecturer in the faculty of Architecture Engineering at the University of Sharjah in the United Arab Emirates. The leap, although big on paper, was like a lovely mountain ride and a view where the road is clear and the weather is breezy, but the end is unknowable. One could reach the beach or the dumpster, and only by arriving know the result of the decision. I was lucky to find myself on the beach, teaching creative thinking, idea generation, design process, as well as leadership skills. One of the tangible results of this trip that links back to my studies at the ICSC was a paper written explaining how I used the Torrance Incubation Model in creating and implementing a course in Design Leadership for graduate architect students (Taher, in press).

My encounters with large-scope projects and the mentality I gained from my studies in extending the learning, stretching my comfort zone, and creating ripple effects, found its way to other clear and salty waters. While CITY Leaders might be one of the biggest accomplishments so far in my career, it's not the only one. "My Arabic Story" lived and thrived for three years beforehand in Montreal, as a storytelling and puppetry powerhouse that shared original, rich, and colorful tales for children and adults alike.

In the aftermath of completing the degree and restarting my career as a creativity and innovation catalyst, I began experimenting with paper and bookbinding, starting my own line of handmade calendars and notebooks. "YomiCal" gave me great pleasure as it was the first tangible product I experienced since I learned about creative products definition back in school. As I look back, eight years after graduation, I can see traces of my studies in the next wave I am riding, starting my next adventure in innovation facilitation and consulting.

Come to think of it, all of this came from one year of intense studies in the distance program at the ICSC. Yes, one year only, and as far as I know, I still hold that record. Drop me a line if you were able to beat me in this and we shall set our next challenge.

References

Amabile, T. M. (1996). Assessing the work environment for creativity. *Academy of Management Journal, 39*(5), 1154-1184.

Lauer, K. J. (1994). The assessment of creative climate: An investigation of the Ekvall Creative Climate Questionnaire. [Unpublished master's thesis.] Buffalo, NY: Buffalo State, State University of New York.

Meyers-Levy, J. & Zhu, R. (2007). The influence of ceiling height: The effect of priming on the type of processing people use. *Journal of Consumer Research, 34* (August), 174-186.

Taher, R. (2008a). *Designing a creative leadership program.* [Unpublished Master's project.] Buffalo, NY: Buffalo State, State University of New York. Retrieved from http://digitalcommons.buffalostate.edu/creativeprojects/125

Taher, R. (2008b). *Inventions and discoveries in the Islamic Golden Age through the lens of Ekvall's 10 dimensions for creative environments.* [Unpublished manuscript.]

Taher, R. (2008c). Organizational creativity through space design. *Proceedings of the 2nd Creativity and Innovation Management Conference* (pp. 209-224). Buffalo, NY: International Center for Studies in Creativity.

Taher, R. (in press). *Combine and synthesize: A case study in design leadership.*

Torrance, E. P. (2006). *The manifesto: A guide to developing a creative career.* Charlotte, NC: IAP.

The Best Use of Time

Maureen Vitali

*C*reative studies? What a waste of time! My goal is to get a job when I get out of here, not waste time studying artists.

I remember these thoughts flashing through my 18-year-old mind as I walked through the SUNY Buffalo State library. I had just been approached by what I deemed to be a man with no basis in reality. The man was waving pamphlets in the air as he excitedly told anyone who would listen that they should minor in Creative Studies, because it would *change their lives*.

I never dreamed that he was right. Now, five years later, I've found that he was!

It was the urging of a trusted co-worker that finally got me to put my skepticism aside and take a Creative Studies course. I remember feeling extremely intimidated as I looked over the syllabus. I toyed with the idea of backing out when I read that I would be expected to create a product that was new and useful. *How am I supposed to do that? I'm not even creative!*

I couldn't be happier that I took that class. I gave Creative Studies a chance, and it has paid off. I did more than minor in Creative Studies: I have joined the ranks of just over 500 students with a Master of Science in Creativity.

People often ask me what I could possibly do with a degree in creativity. I explain that it is more than what this degree will *allow me* to do, but also what I have *already done* with it, and what the *degree has done for me*.

I have gained the knowledge of how to apply research-backed methods to deliberately cultivate innovation, drive positive change, and maximize potential in individuals and groups. Since I began as a student of creativity three-and-a-half years ago, I have had the pleasure of being involved in more than 60 applied creativity sessions. This means that, for each of these sessions, I have used creative tools and processes to assist clients in discovering new and useful ways to determine and accomplish their goals.

Here are a few examples:

I helped New Balance develop an innovative campaign to empower kids to be more active. I conducted professional development sessions with over 180 medical personnel to better equip them to serve their patients; devised approaches to raise awareness and profits for numerous businesses; and mediated heated conflicts with unprecedented success. I have helped aspiring entrepreneurs formulate business plans; aided college administrators in increasing student satisfaction with campus life; and helped school children to leverage their strengths in group-work. I have collaborated with brilliant people worldwide, and have learned from experts in business, education, advertising, and more.

All of this, before I had even graduated!

Since studying creativity, I've lived a life that is passionate, fun, and fulfilling. I work better in groups, have learned to maximize my unique strengths and to embrace the ever-changing world I once feared.

I have learned that creativity is a natural and necessary tool to catapult humanity forward, and that my ability to embrace it has and will continue to lead to my success—both on a personal and professional level.

Now I know that studying creativity is far from a waste of time. Rather, it's the best use of time.

Awakening Adult
Creative Potential

Marta Davidovich Ockuly

For me, teaching creativity is a calling. I've done it, in one shape or another, throughout my adult life. As a child, I played "teacher"—but the job I observed my teachers doing over twelve years of schooling was not what I had in mind. I wanted more hands-on creativity, so I moved in the direction of a career in advertising and marketing with an undergraduate degree in Writing for Radio and Television. Looking back, I don't recall any discussions of creativity in those courses. It was more about developing the skills of copywriting and unique selling propositions for potential clients. I was successful and won awards for my creative work. But with the nineties came corporate takeovers and I opted out of the corporate world with a golden parachute. From that point on, I charted my own creative course.

From founding an alternative advertising agency, a Center for Creative Change, and finally a consultancy called Creativity-on-Call, I could not help but notice how many people were asking me for help connecting with their own creativity and more meaningful work. In response, I developed and taught a course titled: *Career Redirection and Empowerment: Tuning Into Your Passion and Purpose*, which helped participants access joy through creative action. I observed that the people who got *unstuck* were the ones who got out of their comfort zones and took creative risks, which included engaging in different forms of creative expression.

This planted a desire in me to formally study creativity and expressive arts. After earning my Master of Science in Creativity at SUNY Buffalo State's International Center for Studies in Creativity in 2011, I began pursuing a Ph.D. in

Psychology and Creativity at Saybrook University. I've been teaching a course I developed called *Creative Process—Awakening Creative Potential for Personal and Professional Growth* at Eckerd College in St. Petersburg, Florida, for the past five years. I also completed my certification in Person-Centered Expressive Arts with Dr. Natalie Rogers in April 2015.

To this day, I am not a "traditional" teacher. I am a creativity awakener, an encourager of expressive risk-taking and engagement in personally pleasurable creative processes. I inspire curiosity and create safe places for adult learners to play with possibilities. I am a guide through unexplored territory, which unlocks doors to creative potential, which may have been closed for years. I spark imaginations and invite mindful attention to what calls for attention and feels like fun to pursue. I fan the flames of passion for a cause, idea, or question which won't be ignored, and give you permission to play with it. I model a path which offers infinite choices and a compass to assure you are pointed in the direction only you were born to explore. I ask for your trust as we enter a contract, which offers psychological safety, a nurturing environment, and a full honoring of your personal process and preferences. This work requires courage, tolerance of ambiguity, thinking in new ways, openness to different ways of seeing and thinking, and setting aside judgment.

I have learned the rewards for those who step into the river of creative flow can be transformational. My job is done when I see a creative spark lighting up my students' eyes and they suddenly *own* the awareness: *"I am creative."* With that declaration, a torch is passed to that person to light the way for another. I provide the tools, techniques, language, and hands-on experiences to change one's brain and attitude, and turn old challenges or blocks into stepping stones. Students leave my class feeling confident they can use creativity in every aspect of their lives. They end the day exhausted yet energized, rather than depleted and defeated. This is what teaching creative process for personal and professional growth does for me and my students.

What's your burning desire? Whatever it is, a creative education will give you tools to help achieve it. The world is waiting for what you came to Earth to contribute!

A Path to Radical Aliveness

Catherine Tillman

I did not pursue a Master of Science in Creativity in order to get a job or get a raise or make the world a better place. I signed up because both of my grandmothers lived into their 90s, and since I was 57 when I applied, I figured the odds of my living another thirty or so years were good. I wanted to find a way to make the rest of my life the best of my life.

I did not choose to enter the Creative Studies program at SUNY Buffalo State because I thought I would find all the answers. I chose it because I had attended two Creative Problem Solving Institute (CPSI) conferences, and the people I encountered were some of the most intelligent, authentic, and *radically alive* people I had ever met. One of the most impressive was Sid Parnes, a founder of the conference and the Creative Studies program. Whatever it was these people had, I wanted it. The common denominator was that many of them held a degree in creativity from the International Center for Studies in Creativity at Buffalo State.

I was not excited to learn that the program I was entering at the ICSC was offered as a Master of Science degree. The only subject I disliked more than science was math; I would have much preferred the School of Education or Liberal Arts. I was also of the opinion that creativity defied scientific investigation. I emerged from the program, however, with a newfound appreciation for scientific research, and a newly-discovered affinity for neuroscience and neuropsychology. This was the beginning of my ongoing love affair with the complexities of the brain and the mysteries of consciousness, and their relation to the creative process.

Based on scientific studies related to the creative brain, I have changed my diet, my exercise program, my sleep patterns, and the way I relate to my grandchildren. Based on creative education theories and accelerated learning practices that were introduced in the program, I have altered the way I teach and the way I prepare presentations. I continue to follow research in these areas, always looking for practical applications.

When I started the program I had no interest in the current trend toward mindfulness, but as a result of a class assignment, I became immersed in the work of the Harvard professor and social psychologist Ellen Langer. Sometimes called the mother of mindfulness, Langer has been researching the topic for more than four decades. In addition to reading all of her books and much of her research, I attended a weekend workshop she presented. I found mindfulness to be the one of the most transformative concepts I have ever encountered, and a key component to authentic creative expression. As a result, mindfulness is now a central practice in my life.

Based on what I learned about the relationship between mindfulness and creativity, I developed, tested, and launched OwningORANGE, a personal improvement program that provides education and practical exercises for people interested in discovering their creative potential, and in leading more authentic lives.

As I write about authentic lives, I am reminded of my friend Vicci Recckio, who was in my cohort and became one of my dearest friends (another program benefit). Neither of us could have imagined that shortly after she completed her degree, she would be dealing with a cancer diagnosis and years of treatment. In the midst of this challenge, she used tools and techniques she learned in the Master's program and created a product to solve a problem: she launched a company that offers stylish totes in which cancer patients can transport their portable chemo treatments. I know that her creativity helped her during her struggle. Vicci did not survive her cancer, but her business vision will (cosmedicdesigns.com), her creativity continuing to help others.

I have two young grandsons and a granddaughter, and as a grandmother and educator, I am interested in passing along tools for creative thinking to their generation. To that end, I am writing books that introduce concepts in creative thinking to children, and I am working with ICSC Press as a potential publisher.

As I age, I am becoming more aware of our culture's negative attitudes towards aging, and I am concerned about the mental and physical challenges that often characterize an aging population. To address these concerns, I am developing a blog for seniors that introduces current research related to aging, and that fosters the development of the characteristics of E. Paul Torrance's "Beyonders."

Although I did not pursue a Master of Science in Creativity in order to get a job or get a raise or make the world a better place, the knowledge I gained has become a gateway to all three. And although neuroscience, mindfulness, support group facilitation, writing books for children, and dealing with cultural perspectives on aging were not specific curriculum topics, the program provided the framework, flexibility, and support I needed to find my own way to these special interests, and to forge my own path to creative contributions.

I am convinced that what I learned at ICSC will continue to serve me in every situation, no matter how many years I live, or what challenges life may bring. Now, rather than attempting to make the rest of my life the best of my life, I focus on making this moment the best moment of my life. Thanks to my Master of Science degree in Creativity, I have the ability to see infinite possibilities, and the tools to break the patterns that keep us, in Ellen Langer's words, "sealed in unlived lives." What could be more creative than that?

Part 2:
Careers & Callings

Creativity as a Competitive Advantage

Shane Sasnow

Creativity is everywhere. It is in everyone's life. Artists, musicians, scientists, and businessmen are just a few of many who use creativity every day to contribute something valuable to society while enjoying successful careers. What difference does it make to have a degree in it? For me, it provided a career path and a competitive advantage.

At 26 years old I worked as a guitar teacher in Boulder, Colorado. I taught because it was a good way to pay the bills while I worked towards my dream of being a rock star. One day two of the best guitar players in town came into the store where I worked, and I watched as they each expressed their significant unhappiness in unique ways. One was mean. The other was sad. They had both worked incredibly hard and still not found the success they had hoped for. I was about 10 years younger than they were, and I decided on that day that I did not want to end up like that. I refused to become unhappy because my passion for guitar wasn't providing what I wanted: rock stardom, money, fame, women, a living. I told myself that if I wasn't successful with music by the time I was 30 I would go back to school.

In the years following I was very productive, creative, and motivated musically. Unfortunately I couldn't turn that into a living beyond what I could scratch out as a guitar teacher. It was time to shift direction. I went back to school, got multiple degrees, even created my own degree at the University of Washington in creative processes. I studied psychology and philosophy and used them as a lens for understanding compositional techniques in music, art, digital media, creative writing, and design. It was great in many ways, but what I really wanted was a way to make a good living doing something that was interesting and creative. I no longer trusted the music industry because I had seen too many people around me suffer for their musical passion. For a while I tried my hand at being a graphic designer. That was okay but it felt limiting and a bit lonely. Finally I decided to work with people to help them "shine brighter," the way my guitar students did when they made a breakthrough, just at a bigger scale. That led me to get a Master of Science in Creativity at SUNY Buffalo State's International Center for Studies in Creativity.

I pursued the degree so that I could help people be more effective with their creativity and in solving problems. Transferring my creative passion from music and art to helping others solve social and business problems was guided by my study and understanding of creativity as a universal process. I explored my intrinsic motivation and figured out how to shift it from music to people and social systems. I redirected the passion that drives me. Without this shift I would not be happy doing what I'm doing. Without my studies in creativity I would not have been able to make the shift.

People would often laugh when I told them about my degree and ask, "What can you do with a degree in creativity?" At the time I didn't know, but I'd tell them if I couldn't figure something out then the degree wasn't worth much. Turns out it was worth a lot. In the five years since I received my Master's, I have been facilitating groups through creative problem solving processes. Though I probably could have been a facilitator without the degree, the degree has opened many doors. I'm one of a thousand facilitators in my region that can run effective meetings, but I am one of only a few who are credentialed specialists in creative problem solving and innovation. This differentiation has provided me with a significant competitive advantage.

The first good job I got after receiving my Master's in Creativity came from doing a volunteer facilitation for a government transformation organization. We were exploring how an Oregon county might improve its social health system, by discussing how socioeconomically challenged citizens in their county were receiving, or not receiving, adequate health, addiction, and dental care, and how that negatively impacted county services and budgets. At the end of the day, I walked up to the woman who was running the show and told her I was a creativity specialist. Two days later she called and offered me my first consulting job. I went to see her with every book I had on creativity, ready to share everything I knew. She must have been impressed because three hours later she invited me to facilitate a three-day government innovation design lab. The fact that I had both the skills she needed as a facilitator, and knowledge about how to get groups to be more creative and generate innovative outcomes, was what made a lasting impression on her.

Infusing meetings with creative thinking and a bit of fun has consistently made an impression on my clients. Many of them have hired me because they are bored with the usual approach to meetings. I always try to make my meetings interactive as well as productive. An example of my work includes helping a client reimagine how early learning services are delivered in Oregon. As an activity in this workshop, I had participants pretend to be participants of the system they were trying to understand and improve. They took on the roles of service providers, government agents, children, and parents in the early learning system in Oregon, and interacted with each other. By doing this they personalized their knowledge of the system, found places where the system was lacking logistically and emotionally, and were able to generate new ideas and solutions for problems they didn't even realize existed, all while learning and deeply engaging with the process.

Another client hired me to do a full day of creative exploration to come up with something exciting and new in packaging. The fifty design participants were first inspired by images and stories that helped them see things from the perspective of their target market. They were then exposed to ideas, concepts, and behaviors their target market engaged in that had nothing to do with the marketed product, like playing video games or jumping off cliffs. The rest of the time was spent imagining how to make packaging that combined the joy and feelings of the non-product-oriented activities with the product-oriented activities. There were many colorful concepts created that day.

In addition to my work with clients I also use creative thinking methods to solve my own business-development challenges, such as how to connect with the right people to get work, and how to refine my business strategies to fit the available market.

While I went back to college to steer away from musical and artistic creativity, it was my favorite digital audio professor (a musician and artist) who said the thing that inspired me to pursue a Master's in Creativity. He said, "If you can solve people's problems you'll always have work." I took this to heart. It has been the difference between solving my own emotional problems through creative artistic expression (and not making any money) and helping others solve their problems by guiding them through their own creative process—and making a career out of it.

One's Purpose

Russell Schneck

In 2009 I walked away from the comfort and security of a corporate paycheck to embark on a journey with no clear destination in mind. My path would include a Master of Science degree in Creativity from the International Center for Studies in Creativity at SUNY Buffalo State. This experience did not provide a destination, but along with other significant influences, it pointed me in a direction and ultimately changed the course I was on.

My work in the Creative Studies program, particularly my work on the book that was the focal point of my Master's project (Schneck, 2011), put me in touch with what Stanford professor Michael Ray calls the two root questions of creativity: "Who is my Self?" and "What is my Work?" (Scharmer, 2009, p. 164). These questions are referring to one's highest self and one's purpose. And even now, years after earning my diploma and relegating it to a forgotten place within the clutter of my existence, reflections on these questions continue.

My studies reacquainted me with the work of Russell Ackoff and Peter Senge, and in doing so brought systems thinking to the forefront of my perspective. I was first introduced to Ackoff's work in the 1970s, and his interactive attitude of planning (Ackoff, 1974) is at the core of my beliefs. Interactivists want to design a desirable future and invent ways of bringing it about. They believe we are capable of controlling a significant part of the future as well as its effects on us. They try to prevent, not merely prepare for, threats; and to create, not merely exploit, opportunities.

Senge came to my attention in the 1990s with the publication of *The Fifth Discipline* (Senge, 1990), but it is Senge's more recent focus (Senge, Smith, Kruschwitz, Laur, & Schley, 2008) that is most directly responsible for substantially changing the direction of my journey. The developed world is using non-renewable resources at unsustainable rates, generating waste and toxicity in abundance, and in the process expanding social inequities and producing environmental devastation, the most dramatic being climate change. Senge and others in the systems-thinking community are proponents of the "triple bottom line" (Elkington, 1994), a construct that looks not only at *financial* considerations, but *social* and *environmental* consequences as well. Those familiar with the work of Rhodes (the 4 Ps of creativity; 1961) may be intrigued to learn that the triple bottom line is known as the 3 Ps: people, planet, and profits. Considering the views of Elkington and Rhodes in combination, I have 7 Ps defining my concerns.

There was a time I would have said my work was concentrated on organizational creativity. This description remains accurate, but it is inadequate with regard to purpose. After 30-plus years of corporate life, where increasing shareholder value is gospel, quarterly earnings are treated as life and death, and every proposal is evaluated based on how much revenue will be generated or what the cost savings will be, I now advocate that decisions need to be made with different criteria and a broader perspective. Social and environmental consciousness needs to be an essential part of the conversation and the corporate decision-making process. Unless this transformation occurs, the solutions we arrive at today may turn out to be nothing more than tomorrow's problems.

Creativity itself is value neutral, but a creative person cannot be. For me, the challenges facing this country and the world means that creativity includes a responsibility to promote and be a part of the constructive changes that the issues of our time demand.

Social Innovation

When I contemplate my ambition in terms of purpose, it becomes obvious I need to concentrate my efforts on *social innovation*, making a difference where it matters most. The Schwab Foundation for Social Entrepreneurship (2013) defines social innovation as:

> the application of innovative, practical, sustainable, business-like approaches that achieve positive social and/or environmental change, with an emphasis on low-income or underserved populations. (p. 5)

Out of necessity, this focus brings with it a broad definition of how I apply my creativity. I can call myself a consultant, a coach, or a trainer; I do all these things. But the reality is that the initiatives that now inspire me—projects of interest which have the potential to make a positive contribution—require flexibility, versatility, and improvisation. What this looks like in practice is very much a work in progress.

The adage "think globally, act locally" is not only a literal expression of the importance of balancing divergent and convergent thinking: it provides insight about where I can most effectively apply my attention. This directs me to issues of importance to New York's Hudson Valley, where I live. The economy of the region is heavily dependent on agriculture and tourism. Seeing these industries as interdependent rather than separate introduces the concept of agritourism. This concept is directly related to consumer education, typified by farm-to-table initiatives that promote buying local, sustainable farming practices, and healthier eating habits. Family farms epitomize local business, with generational ties to the community, no prospect to move operations off shore, and an inherent concern for the environment. Agritourism celebrates the rich heritage of farming and its importance to the economy. It makes farms, farm stands, and farmers markets a destination not only for fresh fruits, vegetables, and dairy products, but places to learn about the role of farming in society, and to experience one of the remaining segments of our culture not dominated by the mindset responsible for suburban sprawl and the "malling of America" (Kowinski, 1985). Family farms are authentic Americana, but they don't reside in some idealized version of the past that never actually existed; rather, they are vital components of our daily lives in the present, and any business based on products that begin as seeds in the ground always has an eye on the future.

The vision is to create an "economic ecosystem" centered on family farms, their products, their stories, and the societal benefits they provide. An overarching theme of this work is to promote healthy eating through consumer education. Bringing this message to underprivileged communities with unmet nutritional needs is an important objective, and is supportive of New York State's "Healthy Food, Healthy Communities" initiative. But the business-like approach, the actual innovation, is in making consumer education about nutrition and food production, farm-based commerce, and Hudson Valley tourism all part of an integrated strategy intended to expand the potential of what these unified activities can achieve compared to what each can accomplish separately.

The phrase "business-like approaches" from the definition of social innovation highlights an important perspective I am able to offer. I bridge idealism and pragmatism in the form of business plans, project proposals, and grant applications. The financial focus of my corporate experience hasn't disappeared; it is just being applied toward activities where accumulating money isn't the objective but the means to achieving a greater good.

But ideas and plans accomplish nothing unless translated into action. Change occurs only as a result of forward progress, sometimes small and incremental, that more often than not has a foundation in persistence and resilience. The study of creativity has allowed me to appreciate the work of developing and implementing as essential aspects of the creative process (Puccio, 2002). Peter Drucker said it best: "Plans are only good intentions unless they immediately degenerate into hard work." The need to find a way to make progress is always there. This is the work of change.

Conclusion

I look for possibilities and I try to get others to see possibilities; I consider this my job description. The challenge in this is exposing the self-imposed limits on thinking that restrict the possibilities we are able to recognize (Ackoff & Vergara, 1981; Argyris, 1990). I am a provocateur; I try to provoke new ways of thinking. I am also a facilitator, an instigator, and an activist. I network, I listen, and I connect—ideas with ideas, people with new and unfamiliar concepts, and people with people who share common interests. Creativity resides in these connections. The function of process is to access these channels to help people see and think differently in order to actualize change. Michael Ray's root questions—"Who is my self?" and "What is my work?"—highlight the most vital connection of all, to fully connect with one's self and one's purpose. Anyone familiar with Maslow's hierarchy of needs will see the direct relationship to self-actualization, as well (Maslow, 1987).

The journey I began in 2009 was not concerned with a destination, nor is it still. It is driven by purpose. I will conclude with the phrase Daniel Kim (2010) used to end his keynote at the Systems Thinking in Action Conference to emphasize our responsibility for shaping the world of tomorrow: "The future is watching us."

References

Ackoff, R. L. (1974). *Redesigning the future.* New York, NY: John Wiley & Sons.

Ackoff, R. L., & Vergara, E. (1981). Creativity in problem solving and planning: A review. *European Journal of Operational Research, 7*(1), 1-13.

Argyris, C. (1990). *Overcoming organizational defenses: Facilitating organizational learning.* Needham Heights, MA: Allyn & Bacon.

Elkington, J. (1994). Towards the sustainable corporation: Win-win-win business strategies for sustainable development. *California Management Review, 36*(2), 90-100.

Kim, D. H. (2010). The third generation leadership challenge. Presented at the 2010 Systems Thinking in Action Conference. Boston, MA.

Maslow, A. H. (1987). *Motivation and personality* (3rd ed.). New York, NY: Longman.

Puccio, G. J. (2002). *FourSight: The breakthrough thinking profile—Presenter's guide and technical manual.* Evanston, IL: THinc Communications.

Rhodes, M. (1961). An analysis of creativity. *Phi Beta Kappan, 42,* 305-310.

Scharmer, O. (2009). *Theory U: Leading from the future as it emerges.* San Francisco, CA: Berrett-Koehler.

Schneck, R. C. (2011). *The organizational creativity actualization model: A book proposal.* [Unpublished Master's project.] Buffalo, NY: Buffalo State, State University of New York. Retrieved from http://digitalcommons. buffalostate.edu/creativeprojects/136

Schwab Foundation for Social Entrepreneurship (2013). *Breaking the binary: Policy guide to scaling social innovation.* Retrieved from http://www. schwabfound.org/content/policy-guide-scaling-social-innovation

Senge, P. (1990). *The fifth discipline: The art & practice of the learning organization.* New York, NY: Currency Doubleday.

Senge, P., Smith, B., Kruschwitz, N., Laur, J., & Schley, S. (2008). *The necessary revolution: How individuals and organizations are working together to create a sustainable world.* New York, NY: Doubleday.

Who Do You Want to Be a Hero to?

Julia Roberts

The very first day of our first graduate course at the International Center for Studies in Creativity at SUNY Buffalo State, we all sat around our tables in Rockwell Hall and listened. One by one, we introduced ourselves. Adults, ages 29 to 59, an even mix of men and women: our cohort.

The level of humor, warmth, achievement and...yes, anxiety...was above average. As it turned out, we were all above average. There were several marketers, a radio personality, a patent attorney, a couple of engineers, a coach, a lawyer/ yogi, some techies, a few art teachers, and an opera singer. As I sat there, I had a realization: we were the former members of our high schools' photography clubs, student newspapers, A/V clubs, debate teams, drama and art clubs. We were the creative nerds, and had we but known better in high school, we could have been one big glorious clique, rather than marginalized factions of creative "weirdos." Here, in our cohort at the ICSC, we were gathered, celebrated and appreciated. We had all found our people.

As the summer's courses began, we slowly unraveled the mysteries of creativity, in groups and in ourselves. Quickly we were thrown into facilitators' roles, beginning to ply the trade of creative facilitation. As facilitators we helped our "client," a fellow classmate, with an actual problem. As members of resource groups, we gave each other hundreds of ideas on ways to improve our businesses, fix our lives, change our communities, and bring Creative Problem Solving (CPS) into classrooms. Facilitating such a creative group was easy; the ideas flowed with the force of a fire hose.

In the following semester, we endured assessments and measures of creativity. As guinea pigs, we subjected ourselves to multiple creative assessments. We knew our FourSight styles, our Kirton Adaption-Innovation (KAI) numbers, our Adjective Checklist profiles, our PEPS environmental preferences, and of course, the granddaddy of all, our Torrance Tests of Creative Thinking scores. Test by test, we got to know our beasts within—the creativity we'd all toyed with, collaborated with, denied, repressed, regretted, and cherished our whole lives. And we were validated as bona fide creative. Never again would we concern ourselves with that nagging question of "Am I creative?" or its partner doubt "Am I creative *enough?*" We knew we were creative, and we learned just where we excelled, and where we could improve. We knew anyone's creativity could be enhanced. It was awesome. It was liberating.

Gifts, and What To Do With Them

A year later, we had earned graduate certificates in Creativity and Change Leadership. After another year or more, many of us earned the full Master of Science in Creativity. What we had, however, was more than a certificate or a degree: we had the been given the gift of our own creativity. We had insight and experience into where and how to apply CPS. And we had a cohort of people to lean on, seek advice from, and collaborate with as we began to determine, each of us with our different backgrounds and interests, what we would do with CPS in the real world.

What does one do with these gifts?

- The gift of awareness and control over your superpower—your own creativity.

- The skill of facilitating others to reach new heights of creative thinking.

- The power to lead others in FourSight and other assessments so that they can know their strengths and struggles within the process; and so that their teams can free themselves of unseen biases and collaborate more effectively.

- The desire to evangelize and free up creative energy in boardrooms, bedrooms (why not?), classrooms and more.

Me? I flailed around a bit. I'm self-employed. People who were sent to the program by their companies had a clear mandate to deploy what they learned when they returned to work. Some got promoted, or changed their job descriptions to include facilitation. Teachers met with their principals to discuss the benefits of the process and the tools to enhance creativity among their fellow teachers and, of course, their students. For those of us who were self-employed, we had to find a way to grow our businesses into offering CPS—or start new businesses.

My self-employment was as a life coach. As is the case for most industries, 20% of the coaches in the world make 80% of the money. I wasn't in the top 20%—not by a long shot. In order to be in the top 20%, you have to be in it to win it, heart and soul. You had to be sure of what you were building, and build your business brick by brick—website, social media, email list, blog, and so on. And these bricks had to construct something that was marketable, attractive, necessary, and perhaps novel. More to the point, building wasn't the endgame: you had to continue to enjoy working in that business. You couldn't continually jump to another idea and start fresh, and hope to get ahead. (There's the rub, for me.)

I had to ask myself, where does CPS fit into my new business? I've been self-employed for most of my adult life, first as a very successful marketing consultant and more recently as a coach. Still, I could go back to my corporate roots, and find clients who wanted facilitations, right? For a while, that seemed like my true path, and also like the most likely to succeed. People have successful businesses facilitating creativity, and I have corporate experience. So I created Lemony Fresh Ideas, found a partner, and began looking for clients.

At the same time...I knew that I love coaching, and I love helping creative people discover their own creative styles and quirks through knowledge of the process and the FourSight assessment. I started a second company, based on my coaching platform, called Decoding Creativity, focused on individuals and very small creative businesses. Decidedly non-corporate.

I intended to run both businesses. In time, both were building slowly. Both seemed to be reasonable paths for success post-graduation for one who is self-employed.

A Screeching Halt

I wrote earlier about knowing one's creative preferences. In the parlance of the FourSight assessment, I am a clear Ideator, someone with a high preference for paradigm breaking. (On the KAI, Kirton would call me "unemployable.") I'm also a strong Developer and Implementor. I'm the author of three books, and have organized a media tour with a sponsor, a publicist, and multiple television appearances up and down the east coast in an RV with my three kids in tow.

What I'm not is a Clarifier. It makes perfect sense, in retrospect, that rather than clarify which business path made the most sense for me from the beginning, it would seem easier to me to launch both. And as with most unclarified propositions, I came to a screeching halt when something which should have been obvious became suddenly apparent to me.

And you'll probably laugh, but one day it struck me as an entirely new problem: how was I going to have the time to market both these businesses? I was looking at a marketing pie—eight ways to market my business—and thought, "I just can't do both."

So how does an ideator clarify? I hate to give up a pet idea, especially after I've been nurturing it awhile. I'd built the Lemony Fresh Ideas website, recruited partners, and spent an optimistic six months anticipating success. I would feel utterly foolish to give it up. Even if I *couldn't* do both (and how could that be proven?), I *wanted* to do both.

My creative struggle has always been to choose among ideas, to clarify, to converge. For me, this was the challenge to keep front and center. Once, during class, a professor said, "Go slow to go fast," and I practically yelped. That was the missing information of my life. Go slow to go fast. I immediately felt urgent attachment to this concept. I knew it could change my life. I joked that I wanted it tattooed on my arm. I was very good (above average, even) at diverging. Could I learn to honor the creative value of converging?

So here I was about a year later, and people all around me were urging me to converge, to do less, to choose. But I was full steam ahead on my two-business concept...with creative writing and a pet radio project on the side...oh, and a family of three and a husband and a household to run. And the need for income, not slowly but quickly.

Clarification

Against my creative preferences, clarification was in order. A classic clarification tool is called "Why? What's Stopping you?" I used the tool with the statement: "It would be great if I could manage both companies."

> Why? *Because I can't be sure which one will succeed.* Why else? *Because I've already put significant time and energy into Lemony Fresh Ideas.* Why else? *Because I have partners for and inherent obligations to Lemony Fresh Ideas.* Why else? *Because it seems like corporations have the money and the need for the help.*
>
> What's stopping you? *Very limited client contacts.* What else is stopping you? *Limited desire to cultivate corporate friends and clients.* What else is stopping you? *Not enough time to do both.* What else is stopping you? *No vendor standing.* What else is stopping you? *Long sales lead time.*

You can see a bias forming in that debate. I was willing to limit myself to one company if it was Decoding Creativity (for individuals), but *not* to just one company if it were to be Lemony Fresh Ideas (corporate facilitation). I didn't know why, but that seemed true. Mind you, I love facilitating and training, but I was having a big disconnect with selling and populating my life with potential corporate clients.

Who do you want to be a hero to?

A new clarifying question popped into my head: *Who do you want to be a hero to?* If I were going to be working on this night and day...if I were to be talking at conventions and social gatherings about who I help and why...then this work had to blend with my identity. *Who did I want to be a hero to?* In the helping professions, this is a critical question. You're giving with your whole heart, so you want to make sure you're giving in such a way as to help the world become what you want to see. When giving is your profession, you let that burst of energy serve your greater life's purpose so that it gives back to you, refills your well. I meditated and wrote on this topic for over four handwritten pages. *Who do I want to be a hero to?*

In the Master's program we had learned to decode creativity and to facilitate others to great creative heights. We had this new superpower. So like Wonder Woman, I had to remember to use my powers for good. This was a critical, elemental question that cut to my very identity and life vision.

Now that I had asked, the answer was easy.

It was not Coca-Cola, or American Express, or HBO, all former clients of mine. I want to be a hero to people like myself who have great creativity, but never read the owner's manual. They could be more effective, productive, and satisfied if they were coached and facilitated in CPS. They could gain their own superpowers by understanding their creative thinking preferences and how that interacts with the process. They could have their own treasure map, in the form of the CPS process model. And they could end their own struggles as they facilitated themselves using tools for each phase of the process.

I would be their superhero, helping them express themselves with more daring, with more power, and with more effect in the real world. And they would become superheroes themselves: the superheroes of our society, the creative people who are willing to state the less obvious, able to make connections and draw our attention to things that need seeing.

I believe the world would be a better place if creative people were enabled, turned on, united and empowered. Like the first time we all met one another at Rockwell Hall, I realized the world would be a better place if creative people were less stigmatized, marginalized, and unsure of how to use their powers for good. Creative people would be significantly helped just by recognizing the value and the particular brand of their own creative contribution.

And so I offer that question, to help you clarify where to take your creativity degree or creative inclination: *Who do you want to be a hero to?*

In fact, there is likely not one right answer, but a "yes, and."

Earlier in my career, the answer was: my family. I wanted to be a hero to the three little people I was raising with my husband. Being a trained brain, strategist, and conceptor for corporate clients helped me serve my family: set up a household, paid for everything, and gave me the flexibility I wanted to be the kind of mom I wanted to be. Now that my kids are older I want my help to reach a bigger sphere, one that's dear to my heart: the individual artists and creators who need to step into the light and empower their voices, insights and points of view. I want to be a hero to people who have something to say, and who can help this world be a better place.

I have gone slow to go fast. I launched DecodingCreativity.com, and I help individuals and small companies with their creative quests. I have one company, one brand—all my eggs in one basket. *And that's a good thing.* It's something I could never have done for myself without the careful, individualized schooling I got in the CPS process, in my own creativity, and in how to make visions into realities that I received at the ICSC.

Part 3:
Business & Organizational Creativity

Creativity Pays!

Steven Martin

Yes, the exclamation point in the title is intentional, and this essay will explain how and why it is merited—if not an understatement. A hint: I have been applying the principles of creativity and Creative Problem Solving (CPS) in the context of 40-plus years of business experience, generating value for clients at the rate of up to $125,000 per hour and $2,000,000 per two-day working session. *That* is the power of creative process combined with industry experience.

This is the story of how I have applied what I learned earning an M.S. in Creativity from the International Center for Studies in Creativity at SUNY Buffalo State as an independent business consultant working to improve the financial stability of businesses around the globe. In other words, my mission has been that of saving jobs. Before I tell you how, let me tell you how I came to be doing this, as I think it may help you on your journey of discovery on how to apply creativity personally and within your organization.

Discovering Creativity

My first industrial operational invention came when I was a summer student during my senior year in college (B.S. in Engineering, 1972). As a result, I was one of only two engineers the company hired the next year during that economic recession. In four years with that company I developed many improvements for the company, and was promoted four times. The mid-seventies brought a move to another company where the cycle repeated itself nine times over 14 years. I helped put tens of millions of new dollars into the bottom line. They paid me well but I wanted more, so I jumped to a high-tech startup as executive vice president and chief operating officer. Talk about exciting times! There is never enough money and always more than enough risk in high-tech. Everyone's problem solving skills were tested on an almost daily basis as we struggled to make enough progress to make payroll.

At that time, with 20 plus years of valuable experience including a portfolio of creativity and innovation, I thought I was pretty hot stuff, especially when it came to seeing what others did not. I looked at one major research project that had been underway and in trouble for a couple of years and at a cost of about $1.5 million, and saw the root cause quite clearly. The problem was that there was a team of Ph.D.s, engineers, and technicians who also thought they were hot stuff. But R&D reported to another company executive, so my opinion did not count. While I boiled, our 2,000-degree furnaces burned cash instead of producing products.

Then I discovered creativity. Or, more accurately, I discovered *the study of creativity* at the ICSC. And while learning about creativity I also learned about my own creative self.

In a two-session seminar run by the Center faculty I learned that my personal creativity style is that of an "innovator," according to the Kirton Adaption-Innovation Inventory. This assessment places individuals on a continuum, with adaptors (those who create within existing parameters) at one end, and innovators (those who create new paradigms) at the other. In fact, on the KAI scale I rate so far from the mean on the innovator side that I am the first to wonder how I ever get anything done other than to generate new ideas. It was no wonder I had spent so much of my career inventing.

I also learned that the coping mechanisms and management skills which I had been honing for years were what allowed me to adapt to the challenges of working with the 95% of the rest of the population who do not share my creativity style preference. It was even more important that I learned how *people* and *process* interact to produce a *product*. As with just about everything involving people and teams, the better the interaction the better the chance of achieving the desired product.

Now hooked on the scientific fundamentals of creativity, I started night school at the ICSC with an eye toward completing the graduate certificate program, which I later did. The punch line for this bit of history is that I took on that $1.5 million dollar two-year problem as a project for one of my classes. I facilitated a one-day CPS session, starting with problem finding, moving to solution finding and ending with implementation (a high level project plan). I stayed out of content and in that seven-hour period I facilitated the process with the team to solve the problem. Yes, the solution was what I expected, but that is not the point. It was *their* solution. They owned it and they implemented it immediately to save the project and stop the hemorrhaging of cash. It was a perfect example of the power of process (CPS in this case) to cut through ambiguity and personal conflict to get to the truth in an effective and efficient manner.

Discovering Freedom

It is usually very rewarding to be a high level executive in a company but every job comes with a price. Early in the morning of July 3, 1997, the president told me that he and the Board of Directors had agreed that I should take on a new strategic role in the business since I had been doing so well running operations, saving the company money and expanding business. I said I would think about it and left for the day. Talking with my wife, my most trusted advisor, we evaluated the offer and applied some CPS tools. The result: on the morning of July 4, 1997, I cleaned out my office, put a letter of resignation on the president's desk, and declared independence.

With no forethought or planning, I had broken the golden handcuffs of a long and successful corporate career and set out in search of freedom. Empowered by a new self-understanding and the confidence that I could solve just about any problem, I applied for the full M.S. program and graduated in the spring of 1999.

My consulting practice gives me the freedom to work or not work as I wish and to pick and choose only those clients who appreciate what I bring to the table and with whom I enjoy working. I now volunteer well over 1,000 hours per year with SCORE to help entrepreneurs and small businesses for free. This is my joy and exemplifies my current freedom.

Creativity Pays! Explained

As a business executive and an engineer I have always been skeptical about business fads, buzz words, in-fashion ideas, and all those nifty things that make their way through business in about an eight- to ten-year cycle. So, having hung out my consulting shingle as a creativity expert and generalist business consultant, I was faced with a dilemma of my own making: How could I justify charging clients tens of thousands of dollars for a service?

I solved the problem by consolidating the focus of my practice from that of being a creativity generalist to that of being a business specialist. My singular promise is that I am a profit-improvement expert and I will deliver a tangible monetized proof of the value of my work within hours of the completion of a one or two-day working event. The model and associated processes are designed to address the harsh realities of business (see: sidebar).

My model is a fusion of CPS, other proven models, and proprietary material developed and proven over my four decades. In brief, I start with a client problem statement of something like this: "How do we improve the profits of our company?" or "How do we reduce the costs of...?" The highest levels of the organization agree to the problem statement in writing. I then facilitate teams through the working sessions to answer the question. The process looks like this:

1. Executives agree to the problem statement, and agree to support the work their teams will be doing during and after the working session by committing resources to them.

2. The teams are selected in concert with top and middle management. Members often meet each other for the first time on the morning of the event.

3. I facilitate the two-day session which includes:

    - making the case for the need to change costs or profits;

    - teaching the sources of cost reduction and profit improvement;

    - learning how to do divergent thinking (creating ideas);

    - learning how to effectively converge (choosing ideas) on the best ideas; and

    - selecting ideas that are then converted into projects and monetized.

The next morning after the session I deliver a report to the client, which includes the entire body of work produced. The following three cases give real-world examples of results. (Note that all identifying information has been removed; all projects have a contractual commitment of confidentiality.) My typical client is $100 million to $1 billion in annual sales, although I have worked with far smaller businesses.

Case Example A: "How do we reduce costs?"

This $500 million per year business was experiencing significant competitive pressure and rising costs of global operations. They wanted to improve profit margins immediately. The chosen approach was to lead eight different business unit teams through five two-day working sessions to attempt to find $8 million in cost reductions. We spent a total of ten working days to accomplish the following at an average return on investment of over $1 million per day.

Total Ideas Generated	Priority Ideas Selected	Number of Projects Written	Projected Annualized Sustainable Value
2,698	201	81	$10,941,000

This worked so well that we did it again the next year with similar monetary results. The client realized that this collaborative approach for identifying, developing, and prioritizing projects created a buy-in at both the operational and executive levels. As a result, resources for implementation were actually made available.

The Harsh Realities of Business

1. The first job priority is to maintain the status quo no matter how often leaders call for change.

2. Most people do not readily create ideas for improvement and when they do, they have no safe place to take them.

3. Great ideas languish for years despite a dire need for them.

4. "We tried that once before and it didn't work" is an oft-heard mantra. Criticism kills ideas and motivation.

5. There is never enough time or money for implementation.

6. Those who speak loudest or carry the biggest management title always win even when wrong.

7. Money talks. Only real financial improvements deserve the application of resources.

8. People are motivated by being part of progress toward meaningful goals but work usually gets in the way of progress.

Case Example B: "How do we improve profitability?"

A 2,500-employee business was experiencing significant pressure from Wall Street investors to improve profits. The president and executive team needed to act quickly and at the same time avoid the cost of a traditional consulting firm. The chosen approach was to lead 249 people from different business unit teams across the country through two-day working sessions to find cost reduction and profit improvement projects. The total first year annualized value of the work generated was estimated to be $14,000,000. The $49.6 million idea pool included a significant dollar value of revenue-related projects in addition to the cost-cutting ideas.

Total Ideas Generated	Number of Projects Written	Projected Annualized Sustainable Value
4,777	133	$49,625,000

The teams were able to demonstrate improvements to costs and revenues within weeks of starting the program. The consulting and training costs were more than paid for in the first working session. Part of the project was to train an internal team to take over after I left so that they were completely independent within six months to carry on with their task of improving the financial well-being of the company. They used the work product from the training as well as new ideas as a source for ongoing improvements.

Case Example C: "How do I improve profitability?"

A family business of less than $150,000 per year in revenues had stagnant profits. I met with the owner in several one- to two-hour sessions over the course of two months and worked him through the same CPS-based process that I use with big clients. The net result was that he increased revenues by about 30% and more than doubled profits within six months. Later, he told me that his life has changed for the better. I did this for free as a part of my volunteer work with SCORE. This type of engagement carries tremendous personal rewards.

Beyond the Numbers

The monetary results of the engagements I have had with clients over the years prove beyond a doubt that creativity pays. They often tell me that engaging in the process has changed their lives and their businesses in a positive way. They are able to make better decisions and to achieve better results when working with others. Understanding the principles of CPS and creativity changes individuals, teams and organizations for the better.

I have continued my personal exploration of creativity as well. The FourSight assessment, which diagnoses personal preferences for stages in the creative process, has helped me to understand how I have adjusted over my career to become more effective with teams and individuals who do not share my strong preference for generating ideas. It has given me the ability to assess preferences and to guide teams and individuals toward goals in a more effective, efficient, and enjoyable manner.

CPS worked for me because it gave me a language and tools with which to communicate and teach. I can now teach others how to create and invent in concert with their own personality style preferences.

Plato tells us to "know thyself." Rhodes tells us that creative product occurs at the confluence of the environment, the process and the person. When we understand ourselves, as well as those around us, through the lens of creativity, we are personally empowered to change our lives. This short story offers insight into how it changed mine. How will you use this power?

From the Bottom Up

Troy Schubert

What an incredible experience! I sat in a sweltering classroom in early June at SUNY Buffalo State. Judging from the circumstances, I should have been miserable. I had slept for fewer than four hours the night before on a too-hard mattress. I missed my family, and the salads I was eating for lunch every day had lost their appeal. But none of that mattered; I was engaged in the exploration of creativity with 23 other young and old adults from around the world in the Creative Studies program at the International Center for Studies in Creativity.

In reflecting on my experience, there were several factors that made it impactful and galvanizing:

The professors. They were clearly knowledgeable and talented but I found something deeper. They embodied the creative principles they taught and not in a plastic way that tries to shout for your attention. They held the principles in a subtle, authentic, nurturing way that pulled me closer.

The students. They were from around the world, and their resumes were impressive. As the week drew on, they became so much more than their credentials; they became people who touched me with their humanity, and became cheerleaders when I battled my own humanity.

The content. I have been in creative environments for the better part of two decades, in the realm of product development. In spite of this, I was learning new tools and new ways of thinking to build my creativity and nurture it in those around me.

The possibilities. Considering the tools and their applications to my life, a swirl of possibilities began to develop. How might I use this at work? What will this do to my career? What might this mean for my family? What if I were this engaged at work? Better yet, what if I could create this kind of environment for other people at work?

This last question resonated deeply for me. How could I do that? I am a lower-level manager in an organization with more than 4,000 employees. The average tenure is three times my current stay at the company. The thought of taking it on freezes me in fear. But that deep resonance occurs again and I am not sure if I have the idea or if the idea has me. I knew I could get past the fear and I committed to making steady and meaningful progress. What would I do? This paper outlines how I might transform my company...from the bottom up.

Setting the Stage

In the shoe industry, we are squeezed in every direction. Rising costs in China have forced us into third world countries, chasing cheaper labor rates. But these countries (Vietnam, Indonesia) caught on quickly and raised their wages at unprecedented rates in 2012. Pressure from Goliath-sized competition weighs heavily as they lock up intellectual property in some of the most forward-thinking areas of development.

The confluence of rising labor costs and a saturated marketplace has brought a slow realization that dramatic action is needed if the health and vitality of the company is to remain unbroken. The primary response is a reactionary one: What are all of the factors that could incrementally move us forward? Just to name a few: PPH (pairs per hour), labor rate, and key performance indicators. Can we take those dials and just turn them up? There is a limit on those returns. Turning the same old dials to a new higher "maximum" is one way to approach the challenge. But what other options exist? What other dial is hidden from our view? How do we get access to the parameters that affect that dial?

I assert that the hidden dial is creativity. Like many companies, we include innovation as a key organizational strategy but we don't have a holistic, systems-level view of how it works. Thought leaders in the area of creativity offer a model (e.g., Puccio, Murdock, & Mance, 2007) but leaders in my organization are unaware. Our efforts to truly manage creativity are untapped.

Armed with some basic knowledge and a deep sense that this is the answer for the challenges that our organization faces now and in the future, how might I get the message out? What might be all the ways to reach every person in the organization to make this message clear? Beyond just informing them, how might I inspire them?

Day Three

Some warned me about "re-entry." After bathing in the rich, nourishing air of the learning environment at Buffalo State, students are thrust back into the barbed reality of normal life. My re-acclimation seemed uneventful—until my first conversation with Jennifer, a designer with talents that make her especially suited for scoping out the front end of projects. This is where the big thinking occurs, and she is gifted at painting the broad vision. I shared some thoughts from my experience at Buffalo State. I think I might have drawn some circles and asked a couple of open-ended questions. Her eyes lit up and we both saw a clearing for what the project could be—much more expansive than either of us could have envisioned on our own. At the end of the meeting, she pushed back from the table and with a softened gaze took a long pause. Finally she said, "Gosh, I really like the way you're thinking. I have a lot of new ideas from this."

Reflection

In a seamless and natural way, I had adopted a new component in my leadership through my education in creativity. Puccio et al. (2007) stated, "Effective leaders embody the spirit of creativity" (p. xii). Frazier (2013) eloquently adds, "To embody the spirit of a quality suggests a sense of being positively saturated with it in a way which informs not only behavior, but instills a distinct way of being, self-evident to those who witness it" (p. 77).

I had internalized the principles of creativity in a subtle, authentic, nurturing way that was pulling people closer. The mechanism seems to operate by first getting connected with another human being. In the warmth of the exchange, our guards drop. We stop thinking of protecting ourselves just long enough to let a dream slip out.

Digging Deeper

And so it continued to build like this. One conversation at a time, I began to feel my environment shifting and my confidence building. Fueled by my wins, I started to get more serious about how I could have influence. What else might I do to move the needle?

Rhodes (1961) defined creativity on four levels. Each level has a unique identity, but functionally they operate as one:

- Person: characteristics of creative people

- Product: artifacts of creativity

- Process: how people create

- Press: the climate in which people create

If I brought the four strands of creativity into focus to make an impact in each of these areas, I felt that I could make meaningful progress toward creating an environment that might begin to mirror the atmosphere I experienced at Buffalo State.

Day Nine

I facilitated a post mortem on a project called Genesis over lunch. We rarely hold such events; in fact, I have never attended one in the four-and-a-half years of my tenure. However, I had a sense it would make a difference for the team. Within our organization, the Genesis project had been cast as a failure. For our six-member team, it was a two year investment of time, money, and effort that culminated in no revenue. I scheduled the post mortem after my Day Three conversation with Jennifer. We were apprehensive to "go big" on the new initiative because we wanted to avoid the same failure from Genesis.

I decided to use an evaluation tool I learned at Buffalo State in which the positive aspects are identified first, before any issues (problems or negatives) are discussed. It was a good choice.

During the post mortem, a deep sense of appreciation and pride emerged as we focused on the positive aspects of the project. We got in touch with the moments that were deeply meaningful to us. It was interesting and illuminating how each person on the team had a unique perspective on the project.

Moving to the issues, emotions began to heat up. One challenge we faced during the project was being married to a factory development partner who had no belief in the initiative. During a typical alcohol-fueled dinner party with this factory partner, one of the leaders of their group held up a liquor bottle and said, "Hey, it's [shaped] just like the Genesis project...a bomb!" It was funny on the surface. But over the course of the project, this attitude was the underlying problem that gave rise to hours of conference calls and detailed tracking in an attempt to babysit this "strategic" partner. I saw Rachel's face turn beet red as she relived the events at the dinner party. I tried to remain objective but the metal taste in my mouth told me that I was sharing the same gush of adrenaline.

Reflection

I felt like a therapist after this session. Or more accurately, like a healer. In fact, before the post mortem, one of the members of the team actually said, "Why are you doing this—to open up old wounds?" In preparation for the meeting, I had people bring something from the project that had particularly strong energy for them. I have no doubt that reconnection with these physical objects stirred up some of the suppressed emotions.

Digging Deeper

I had a sense that the negative thoughts, feelings, and pain of embarrassment from the unsuccessful project were having a limiting effect on the team's ability to apply new thinking on the future initiative. The post mortem's healing effect, I thought, might provide a clearing in which we could engage with the new project. This approach is validated by research that shows how emotions and the affective system are an integral part of creativity (Amabile, 1987; Torrance, 1972). Presented in this way, the approach makes intuitive sense. But how do we know when negative emotions are limiting creativity? Through mindfulness, we can know this. I had somehow become saturated with this trait as well.

Once I had mindfully reflected on the situation, it took courage and empathy to take further action. I had provided a space where people could express their disappointments, something rarely done in the work setting. Who wants to expose their vulnerability on this level? And further, who would want to lead people through it? The answer: someone who is committed to the creative effort. I acknowledged the role I played in the post mortem and I also acknowledged my team for trusting me to lead them there.

Day Ten

After the post mortem, I worked with my manager to converge and cluster on the key issues that were revealed. Using a technique from the Creative Problem Solving toolkit, we restated the clusters into challenge questions (forward-thinking questions, often beginning with the phrase "How might...") that state issues in a way that invites creative solutions. In addition to factory partner issues, another challenge was how we might build and sustain a strong relationship with marketing. This has been a source of frustration since the team's inception three years earlier.

I emailed Rick, VP of Marketing, and he agreed to meet with me. I told him we were having challenges on the team and hoped that we could get to the bottom of the conflict. The meeting was productive and enlightening for both of us, marking the first time I had ever reached out directly to Rick. (My manager, VP of Innovation, usually managed the relationship with marketing.) Rick was calling for a more collaborative relationship with the innovation team. At the same time, we were trying to push them away so we could focus on our work. After the meeting, I pulled together our core team, including my manager, and told them we were meeting with Rick, together.

At the start of the team meeting with Rick, I carefully detailed the meeting objectives on a flip chart and made sure we were all aligned. Throughout, I documented our progress with Post-its and kept us moving forward. At the end, when we had accomplished our goal, Rick was visibly excited. We were all present at the creation of a unified vision for how we might partner. Rick said, "This is the best day I've had at work in a long time!"

Reflection

I find that we make so many assumptions about what others want and expect. It can be a source of tremendous confusion and waste. Getting into dialogue is the only way to make progress. It requires generous listening and a faith that a win-win solution exists.

Digging Deeper

I have had a wonderful relationship with fear throughout my life: when it talks, I stop and listen. But the results I produced above suggest that I have transcended fear in some way. I'm pointing to the fear of what my manager might think as I schedule a meeting and talk directly with another VP (Rick). Fear of repercussions has certainly stopped me in the past.

Now transcended, the fear is exposed in its true colors: it is an indulgence that gives me the justification to walk away. If I look long enough at the fear and peel back the layers, I see what Williamson (1992) spoke of when she said, "our deepest fear is not that we are inadequate...our deepest fear is that we are powerful beyond measure." Once in touch with this reality, it becomes clear why I would indulge in fear: it keeps me from evolving and growing to the next level where I could really make a difference.

Walsch (1995) provided another perspective on how I had moved past fear: "You will set aside these things [this fear] as a child sets aside toys. Not because they are unworthy, but because you have outgrown them" (p. 96). I would assert that I've outgrown the fear of success on some level. This is a breakthrough for me.

Day Eleven

An opportunity opened up to attend the 2013 Creative Problem Solving Institute (CPSI) in Buffalo, NY. My pre-conference session was led by Andre de Zanger. By turns, he reminded me of Leonardo da Vinci...or Hannibal Lecter. Thankfully, he never once demonstrated cannibalistic tendencies, but he had a raw, primal energy augmented by deep wisdom and piercing insight. I caught him during a break and told him about my efforts to transform my work climate from the bottom up. As the words tumbled from my mouth, I felt a cringe of embarrassment as I read his reaction. After a deep sigh, he turned to me and shared his wisdom. He said quite simply, "You have to get to the pharaoh. It needs to come from the top." His words washed over me like a cold shower. Thoughts like this from any other source might be ignored, but this man was speaking from a place of certainty made sturdy by a lifetime of thwarted youthful exuberance. He seemed tough and unshakable in spirit, but even he wasn't willing to cast an optimistic vote for the underdog.

Reflection

Again, the notion of faith arises. I'm disempowered by what he says and experience a loss of faith as a result. However, I have this innate sense that I should not stop.

Digging Deeper

Going past my initial reaction to his comments, I see he is actually pointing me in a direction that makes sense: go to the leader of the company. In my case, however, this does not make sense because I don't have this kind of access at my level within the company.

Day Seventeen

I've been participating in a leadership training program called Pinnacle Leadership. The program is designed for top performers across the company who show promise in becoming the future leadership. This was our final session in a nine month program. We were to present innovative ideas about how we might move the company forward. I chose to talk about the possibility of an upward shift in the innovative culture and prepared a talk to show the gap that exists between our current state and an ideal culture of innovation.

Some background is required to paint a clear picture here. I had missed the previous session where everyone else presented his or her ideas, so I was the only one presenting on this particular day. Also, at the last session, I learned that an overwhelming sense of pessimism had emerged upon the completion of the presentations. The team realized the value of their creative ideas but was deflated because they had a sense that nothing would move forward in the organization's current climate.

When I gave my talk, I presented Rhodes' (1961) creativity construct (person, process, product, and press). I then had the group rate each facet of creativity on a scale from one to ten. I used an ad hoc math equation stating that the creative potential of the ideal company is 10 x 10 x 10 x 10 = 10,000. When we rated ourselves, we got a score of 5 x 6 x 1 x 3.5 = 105. We were realizing 105/10000 = ~1% of our creative potential!

Reflection

The talk generated considerable excitement. Suddenly the group recognized how all of their ideas could become possible inside the fulfillment of a more innovative climate where creativity is nurtured and fostered.

We discussed how to move forward. The team wanted me to present my ideas at the graduation ceremony the following morning, which included all of the cohort's managers and members of the senior leadership team including the company CEO.

I had reached the pharaoh.

Digging Deeper

Consulting with Dr. John Cabra at the ICSC, he directed me to literature on more legitimate ways to assess the creativity of an organization. Kerle (2012) provided an overview of creativity assessment from a systems view, discussed data gathering methods, and examined a measure called MIX (Management Innovation Index). These researchers were fueled by the notion that measurement is critical to understanding and managing creativity, giving credibility to the field of creativity and moving it from a mystical entity into a science.

Day Eighteen

In the end, we agreed that I would not give my full presentation at the graduation ceremony as it was not the right forum for pushing any agendas forward. Instead I prepared a two minute "teaser" talk to capture the essence of my vision. I practiced it until it was buttery smooth. I videotaped myself and played it back. I added just the right pauses. It was perfect.

We had a rich discussion at the ceremony with my leadership team (nine of us), our managers, CEO Rob Brancato, and other members of the senior leadership team (probably 35 in attendance). When it came time to talk about the innovative culture in our organization, the group turned it over to me. I pushed play on my teaser talk, asked some open-ended questions and then finished up. Immediately after I stopped talking, Rob said, "How do we follow up on this? This needs to get on my calendar." I found out later that we (the leadership team) would have four hours with him to talk about our ideas. The energy was electric. What an amazing result!

Reflection

I was ten minutes late for the meeting that morning. I was lucky in that I missed very little and was able to stop beating myself up almost immediately. The lesson here was to keep my feet on the ground and manage my integrity; it was great to have the attention of the CEO, but I had to manage my commitments and not lose myself in the excitement.

Digging Deeper

In honesty, my excitement and passion had been the primary catalysts propelling me forward to this point. I used some tools and background theory, but a future visit with the CEO would certainly require a new level of rigor, articulation, and confidence.

Going forward, my plan is to present shortly and sweetly during the four-hour session, and to provide Rob with a take-away document for further review and understanding of my thinking. I'll make myself available if he wants to talk more.

After the graduation ceremony, Rob caught up with me outside the conference room. He leaned in as we approached each other and shook my hand. He thanked me for my commitment. I expressed appreciation for him listening to what I had to say. The rest was random small talk, but his authenticity and selflessness was clear in his drive to make our company extraordinary. I am with him in that.

Insights

In reflecting on what I have accomplished in 20 days since exiting the ICSC summer session, I would like to try to articulate what made the most significant impact on me.

What's the best possible outcome?

In a class assignment, I shared an insight where I confessed that it is my natural tendency in approaching new situations to: (a) imagine the worst possible outcome, and (b) actively recruit defensive actions and behaviors to avoid that worst possible outcome. This mindset provides protection from disaster but leaves little space for generating meaningful results. I invented a new vantage point called "What is the best possible outcome?" This is a very different trajectory. Living with this insight contributed to the results I produced.

Who I Want to Be...

I am often confronted by the resistance that shows up around me, whether resistance to change or resistance to something new. I recoil from it or resist it. Again, I found inspiration in Walsch (1995) when he wrote:

> And forget not Who You Are in the moment of your encirclement by that which you are not. But do you praise to the creation, even as you seek to change it. And know that what you do in the time of your greatest trial can be your greatest triumph. For the experience you create is a statement of Who You Are—and Who You Want to Be. (p. 34)

On several occasions, I read this passage to myself and it brought strength and reassurance.

My Personal Press

I created a mini-climate from my community at the ICSC. I owe tremendous thanks to Katie Haydon and Doug Reid. They believed in me more than I believed in myself. They gave their time, energy, and love to me and placed no limit on where I could take this. They were not even surprised when I reached the CEO because they saw the potential in me from day one. I am lucky to have such friends and hope that I can someday pay it forward. In some ways, I doubt that I could ever be so generous, but Katie and Doug would certainly have something to say about that. Dr. John Cabra has already begun supporting me in preparing for my meeting with Rob. I thank him in advance for his time, passion, and intellect.

Conclusion

The question as to whether a low-level manager in an organization with over 4,000 employees could transform his organization has not been answered. As Andre de Zanger would say, I have reached the pharaoh, so it may be possible. I make no promises, but the trail I have forged has been an inspiration to my team, my manager, and others around me as they watched me grow. In fact, I may have even inspired the CEO of my company. The question of why study creativity becomes self-evident when one does it—sometimes in as little as 20 days.

References

Amabile, T. M. (1987). The motivation to be creative. In S. G. Isaksen (Ed.), *Frontiers of creativity research: Beyond the basics* (pp. 223-254). Buffalo, NY: Bearly Limited.

Frazier, A. (2013). What are the natural relationships between creativity and leadership? In C. Burnett & P. Reali (Eds.), *Big questions in creativity 2013*. Vol. 1 (pp. 69-88). Buffalo, NY: ICSC Press.

Kerle, R. (2012). How can creativity become a tangible process and a prime contributor to the strategic objective of the organization? Retrieved from http://www.ralphkerle.com

Puccio, G. J., Murdock, M. C., & Mance, M. (2007). *Creative leadership: Skills that drive change*. Thousand Oaks, CA: Sage.

Rhodes, M. (1961). An analysis of creativity. *Phi Delta Kappan, 42*(7), 305-310.

Torrance, E. P. (1972). Can we teach our children to think creatively? *The Journal of Creative Behavior, 6,* 114-143.

Walsch, N. D. (1995). *Conversations with God: An uncommon dialogue*. New York, NY: G. P. Putnam's Sons.

Williamson, M. (1992). *Return to love: Reflections on the principles of "A Course in Miracles."* New York, NY: HarperCollins.

Musings on Creativity Applications in Business

Josh Mahaney

Creativity and Janusian Thinking

One of my favorite mythical figures is Janus, the Roman god of beginnings, ends, and transitions. He is usually portrayed facing in two opposing directions, indicative of his ability to see both the future and the past simultaneously. The psychiatrist Albert Rothenberg theorized about the creative process, borrowing the concept of Janus to coin the term "Janusian Thinking." Rothenberg (1971) defined this way of thinking by adopting the Janusian reality—simultaneously conceiving two contradicting or opposite ideas—and linking it to the creative process. When I first studied creativity, one of the first concepts raised was the notion that everyone is creative. We all create. Therefore, is it not Janusian, or contradictory, to have a degree in creativity?

The theoretical argument for a degree in creativity has more merit when deeper examination validates that creativity is trainable (Scott, Leritz, & Mumford, 2004). When it comes to businesses, creativity is ostensibly a highly-desired skill. One needs look no further than IBM's (2010) global study of more than 1500 CEOs from over 60 countries and 33 industries worldwide, which concluded that creativity is the number one leadership competency for the future. In my experience, and in that of many other professional colleagues I've interviewed, creativity is a very Janusian topic in business. On one hand, creativity is highly desired in companies. On the other hand, however, the initial financial return on a company's initial creative ideas eventually devolves into an internal environment with a rigid status quo to support the old ideas. This establishment slowly minimizes new creative production over time and creates a risk-averse culture.

My anecdotal experiences are articulated well in Staw's (1995) article "Why No One Wants Creativity," where he argues similarly about why creativity and innovation are systematically rejected in established organizations. The irony compounds when one examines Forrester Research's (2014) study commissioned by Adobe, "The Creative Dividend." The study showed that companies which support creativity experience exceptional revenue growth compared to their peers, greater market share, competitive leadership, and even recognition as being the best places to work. However, 61% of companies surveyed don't see their own as creative.

Creative Process in Business

After examining the apparent contradiction between a company's desire for employees to be creative and a status quo that hinders it, one can find a Janusian tension. The tension created by the desire for a company to be more creative and the struggle to achieve it is an opportunity for applied creativity—and in my case, the application of the skill set and knowledge that comes with a degree in creativity. Whether a client employs an external creativity and innovation agency to come up with ideas, or an organization commences its own creative change internally, or both, the opportunities for creative change in business are vast.

I have had the opportunity to work at the major international entertainment company Disney, assisting in adopting a new innovation process for creative change. The consultancy ?WhatIf! Innovation developed an organizationally-specific innovation methodology intended for company-wide adoption in the global sales and marketing department. A small group of trainers with diverse backgrounds were charged with training the organization in this new innovation process. As a result of my degree, I was able to understand the affective, behavioral, and cognitive creativity tools underlying the ?WhatIf! methodology brought in by these trainers, and ultimately to assist in training and facilitating senior executives through the following years.

The degree in creativity also helped me to gain important insights into how creativity works in big business—and how it does not. I have seen large publicly traded companies attached to short-term earnings performance as a result of investors waiting with bated breath for their quarterly earnings report. These companies emerge with an over-saturated hierarchy where decision making relies on committees engaged in laborious and slow consensus building. Not surprisingly, this structure leads to a hyper-aversion to risk-taking, a preference for incremental changes, and no supportive culture of paradigm-shifting innovation. Of course, large companies also exist that maintain an innovative edge and thrive on long-term investment forecasting, such as SpaceX. Such companies typically have a rare creative leader with a focused long-term vision, empowering employees' creativity to collectively overcome the challenges along the way.

The large companies struggling with innovation present a Janusian opportunity for those with a creativity degree. When an organization's barriers to innovation preclude it from anything but minute improvements, those experienced in applied creativity and innovation can assist. With the degree, one could work for innovation consultancies such as IDEO, ?WhatIf!, or Frog Design to help companies be more creative and innovative, or work on a company's in-house team that has chosen to create a culture of creativity and innovation. Either way, a degree in creativity is a credential that speaks to a specialized skill set differentiable from traditional candidates for the job. In these cases, creativity is attractive and even sexy to those seeking change. Tradition is understandably dismissed.

Creative Process and Perspective

A credential or degree in creativity, in addition to being advantageous to any company trying to be more innovative or to a consultancy in the business of innovation, delivers perspective on process. I have worked professionally with three major creativity/innovation methodologies: Creative Problem Solving, design thinking, and a version of the ?WhatIf! innovation process. Working with these processes, I have been able to see the balancing act between creating a process that is accepted and works and one that successfully delivers net creative outcomes. As a professor once told me, "Ask the question, 'What works for whom under what circumstances?'" When evaluating creative products, social context is essential (Amabile, 1996). And when evaluating an organization's openness to creativity or the introduction of a new creative process, understanding socio-cultural context is tantamount to success.

Creative change and innovation development must involve a careful analysis of the company's organizational structure, noting the way people work with each other and how ideas are accepted and implemented.

I worked at Disney Design Group for their Research & Development Innovation Lab after working to bring the ?WhatIf! Innovation process to Global Sales & Marketing. What worked with hundreds of sales and marketing employees in the same company did not work in my new role. In the R&D role, design thinking was the creative process that best fit the subculture. Its empathy-centered service design methodology fit much better than the collaboration-centric and easily digestible ?WhatIf! process. The CPS process I studied as a graduate student helped me in both roles at Disney. It gave me another tool kit to empower employees and a foundational skill set to understand the "Why?" behind new creative process tools I taught and used. It positioned me as a thought leader in a field where others struggled.

Creativity and the Future

The M.S. in Creativity from SUNY Buffalo State provides an essential skill set for the aforementioned reasons. More importantly, it is a skill set that prepares individuals for the future. A degree in creativity prepares individuals for the future better than any other I've encountered, for two reasons. First, many students go to school for discipline-specific degree programs to tackle domain-specific challenges professionally. A degree in creativity provides a trans-disciplinary way to approach challenges and opportunities. Approaching challenges without an explicit context is very Janusian: open-ended, yet with expectation for applied solutions. The future's grand challenges will need people of a multi-disciplinary nature working together with a trans-disciplinary process like Creative Problem Solving.

The second reason creativity is best suited for the future is the pace of change in industry. Technological change is increasing exponentially (Nagy, Farmer, Bui, & Trancik, 2013) and disrupting whole industries faster than ever before. Take the disruption created by Netflix to bankrupt Blockbuster, digital imaging to bankrupt Kodak, eBay on auctions, Amazon.com on bookstores, Google on research, Uber on taxis, and Airbnb on the hotel industry. These innovative products and services came out of seemingly nowhere to shock the competition. Bartlett (1969) summed up this phenomenon nicely when he said, "The greatest shortcoming of the human race is the inability to understand the exponential." Creativity will be needed in the future to overcome what Christensen (2013) called the "innovator's dilemma," the inability of firms to adopt these disruptive new technologies and stay relevant.

In an increasingly disruptive future, creative thinking will be more and more relevant. A methodology of applied creativity will no longer be a nice-to-have for future creative leaders. It will be an imperative. Janus, I think, would agree.

References

Amabile, T. M. (1996). *Creativity in context: Update to the social psychology of creativity.* Boulder, CO: Westview press.

Bartlett, A. A. (September, 1969). *Arithmetic, population and energy: Part 1* [Video file]. Retrieved from http://www.albartlett.org/presentations/arithmetic_population_energy.html

Christensen, C. (2013). *The innovator's dilemma: When new technologies cause great firms to fail.* Boston, MA: Harvard Business Review Press.

Forrester Research (2014). *The creative dividend: How creativity impacts business results.* Retrieved from http://landing.adobe.com/en/na/products/creative-cloud/55563-creative-dividends.html

IBM Corporation (2010). *Capitalizing on complexity: Insights from the global chief executive officer study.* Retrieved from http://www-935.ibm.com/services/us/ceo/ceostudy2010/

Nagy, B., Farmer, J. D., Bui, Q. M., & Trancik, J. E. (2013) Statistical basis for predicting technological progress. *PLoS ONE, 8*(2): e52669. doi:10.1371/journal.pone.0052669

Rothenberg, A. (1971). The process of Janusian thinking in creativity. *Archives of General Psychology, 24*(3), 195-205.

Scott, G., Leritz, L. E., & Mumford, M. (2004). The effectiveness of creativity training: A quantitative review. *Creativity Research Journal, 16*(4), 361-388.

Staw, B. M. (1995). Why no one really wants creativity. In C. M. Ford & D. A. Gioia (Eds.), *Creative action in organizations: Ivory tower visions & real world voices* (pp. 161–172). Thousand Oaks, CA: Sage.

The Value of Teaching Incubation in Corporate America

Sandra A. Budmark

When asked, most people know the term "incubation" only as it applies to eggs. *That is what happens before chicks hatch, right?* The process of incubation was introduced in another framework in 1926 when Graham Wallas identified a four-step creative process: *Preparation, Incubation, Illumination,* and *Verification*. Wallas described Incubation as "the stage during which he was not consciously thinking about the problem" (Wallas, 1931, p. 80). The concept of incubation in this context has been described, studied, and debated ever since. "The creative process seems to require a process of incubation, when rational, conscious activity is stopped and the unconscious is allowed to work on the problem" (Bird, 1989, p. 43). Torrance recognized the role of incubation in learning, including it in the name of his instructional model, the Incubation Model of Teaching (Torrance & Safter, 1990).

Incubation is a vital process in creative thinking and problem solving for both individuals and teams, yet it seems to be a well kept secret. There might be great value in bringing this critical skill to corporate America. People at work are constantly solving problems. The skill and understanding of the incubation process would be very valuable to them. They would experience less stress and frustration, have a tool for breaking a "log jam" in their thinking, and be able to plan for the process with their teams.

There are three aspects of incubation that would be helpful to understand: what incubation is; how the brain works when incubating; and the signals that indicate the need for incubation (and the openness to the potential "aha" that can result).

By actively engaging in the incubation process rather than being manipulated by it unknowingly, people will find their work more fulfilling.

What Incubation Is

In order to actively use the skill of incubation, people must first know about it and recognize it. During my research I formally interviewed nine people (see Appendix A for interview results) and asked others informally if they had ever heard of incubation in the context of problem solving. Only one person I spoke with had ever heard the term.[1]

Elsewhere, incubation seems to be an unknown. For those who had never heard the term, I asked if they had ever "slept on it" or "given it a rest." Then the light bulb would go on: of course they had done that. When asked if they used this process purposefully, only one said they did. Some said they spent a long time exhausting themselves until finally giving up at a point where a solution seemed hopeless. What a waste of energy! People might avoid the negative feelings that come from frustration and surrender if they understood that after working on a problem for a period of time it is beneficial to put it aside *with the intent to return to it*. The incubating brain will continue to work and one can then return to the problem with positive energy and optimism.

If people don't fully understand the process of incubation, how might they know to use it to their advantage?

The first important step in teaching incubation is helping people to understand it. There are several ways to explain incubation to someone, from simple to complex. Williams (2008) stated simply that incubation allows time between defining the problem and coming up with new ideas, essentially letting the mind do the work to solve the problem. Ayan (1997) wrote a more thorough description of incubation that also highlights the triggers that indicate when to start the incubation process:

> It is often said that the key function of the unconscious mind during this period is connecting ideas. Creativity is the result of your mind's ability to link ideas, producing something new and different. In connecting ideas, the mind is actually performing a variety of processes.... How does your mind know when to move from preparation to incubation? In general, whenever you begin to feel stressed, tired, distracted, or bored, your mind is telling you to take a break and let incubation begin. (p. 41)

---

1 It happened to be my husband, who had learned it in his 20-year Navy career. I was surprised when he correctly described the process to me in some detail. In Buffalo State's Foundations of Creative Learning course, we learned that the military used creative problem solving, and my husband served as evidence of this fact.

Wallas (1931) goes so far as to say it is *necessary* to use incubation, especially on more difficult forms of creative thought. He contended that there should be an interval free from conscious thought and that this interval needs to allow for the free working of the unconscious processes of the mind. When I took the time to explain this process to the colleagues that I interviewed, they all said that it was very helpful to know. They indicated that they would be more likely to give their problem a rest sooner, knowing that it would help them find the solution.

How the Brain Functions During Incubation

The second fundamental understanding of incubation is how the brain works during incubation. When people actively work on problems, they are using conscious mental effort. When using incubation, they let their unconscious minds take over and do the work for them. Ayan (1997) stated that the most important characteristic of incubation is that it happens at the unconscious level, out of active mental control. The brain has the ability to run in the background and process information, similar to the background scans of a computer program. While this processing is taking place, people can do other productive things, or just relax. "Thinking takes physical energy, and by temporarily suspending your conscious efforts to solve some problem, you recharge your mental batteries" (Puccio, Murdock, & Mance, 2007, p. 81). It also appears that we incubate during our dreams:

> Summoning forth your unconscious through a dream is an excellent habit to cultivate. It can contribute to a connection with the unconscious that proliferates in time. Like a river, the unconscious unearths treasures as it continues on its course. When you flow with the creative process, your life also becomes a source of surprises and rewards. (Morris, 1992, p. 105)

This harnessing of the brain's power is essential to finding good solutions to problems. If people do not understand it, corporate America is losing out.

When I mentioned during my interviews that incubation uses the unconscious mind, I could feel the level rising on their skeptical meters. I work with both engineers (generally more analytical) and architects (generally more artistic). Depending on the point of view, pointing out scientific references behind the unconscious workings of the brain can be helpful to validate the idea. For instance:

> In the incubation stage, when the conscious mind is less active, less ACTH [adrenocorticotropic hormone] is secreted. This "downtime" may allow the brain to regenerate the ACTH that ushers forth creative ideas in the illumination stage. The unconscious mind is dominant in the incubation stage, which is when the individual must refrain from focusing on the task or challenge at hand. (Dacey & Lennon, 1998, p. 197)

This scientific explanation of the brain during unconscious activity helps to take the mystery out of the process. After hearing more details about the unconscious mind and exactly how it works to help solve problems, all of the people I spoke with went away with a greater understanding of the process. They seemed much more open to the idea of their unconscious mind working for them.

Signals that Call for Incubation (and the Potential for an "Aha")

The third aspect of incubation that people need to be aware of is their personal signals that they need incubation, and their (related) encounters with "aha" moments. Cultivating these awarenesses has helped me to be much more productive. I no longer fret if I cannot come up with a solution right away because I know that my brain will help me out if I give it a chance. During my interviews when people told me that they waited until they were frustrated to give up, I suggested that if they purposefully stopped working sooner and gave the problem a break, they would avoid the frustration. This idea was novel to them but they admitted they could see the value.

A common question is how long incubation typically takes. One review of experiments on incubation speaks to this question. "Effects of the length of the incubation period depend on whether incubation is short-term or long-term, with maximal effects at 30 minutes and longer periods of 3.5 and 24 hours still resulting in increased incubation effects" (Dodds, Ward, & Smith, n.d., p. 42). Even if time will not allow for an overnight incubation period, as little as a thirty-minute break can be effective. The most important point to take away is that when the triggers of frustration, exhaustion, annoyance, stress, boredom, or tension first appear, set the problem aside and take a break. By understanding and implementing this simple technique, people will be more effective and less stressed.

It is interesting as well to explore the "aha" phenomenon. "Aha" is a potential result of incubation and is directly influenced by it.

> The experience of a breakthrough or "aha" involves an often sudden, usually complete picture of a solution that "comes to us," sometimes even in dreams. Frequently, we cannot explain the cause of the insight, nor explain how we derived it. This numinous or magical quality of the experience results from unconscious work that has gone on. (Bird, 1989, p. 46)

I asked the people during my interviews when they usually had a breakthrough or an "aha" occur. Three said they often wake in the middle of the night with an "aha," another three noticed it while driving. Other responses included while walking or having quiet time, just before sleep, in the shower, and while visualizing things. Morris (1992) provided a possible explanation for this:

Many people fall into dream-like states when they are walking, driving, sailing, floating on water, or engaged in some other lulling activity. These states often seem to be connected with motion. At those times, new ideas are generated, solutions are found. By not remaining stationary, we seem to let go of conscious thinking and allow a deeper, wiser part of ourselves to come forth. (p. 109)

Wallas (1931) contended that the only activity *not* conducive to incubation is reading, because reading stops the ability for the unconscious mind to process.

When people have an aha moment, they need to capture it immediately, if possible, so as not to lose it. Coming from the unconscious, the idea is not in long-term memory yet. "We are, as a rule, unaware of this fact, because we either do not observe or soon forget all mental events outside the limits of full consciousness" (Wallas, 1931, p. 51). Recording an idea right away also helps to remove the stress of trying to remember it, especially if it comes in the night or first thing in the morning when the unconscious is very active. During the interviews, only one person said that he kept a note pad handy to write down ideas. Some said that they emailed or texted themselves, others said that they left themselves voicemails. Some would simply try to remember their ideas. When they understood why the ideas needed to be immediately recorded, they all agreed that this made sense to them. It was not something that they knew or actively thought about. By discussing it with them, they said that they were going to capture their ideas in the future.

Teaching Incubation

In business, as is said, time is money. Teaching the value of incubation does not need to take an inordinate amount of time. A well-prepared one hour class would be sufficient. Convincing department managers to give up their staff for training must always be justified by showing the value. If an individual or team saved an hour a month in time wasted by knocking their heads against a problem, then the time for training would be paid back in 30 days and returned 12 times in a year, a very effective return on investment. A sample lesson plan for teaching the value of incubation is shown in Appendix B. This plan is written using the Incubation Model of Teaching (Torrance & Safter, 1990).

By teaching the use of incubation, individuals and teams would greatly benefit, as would corporate America. There are tangible benefits such as better solutions to problems, more effective innovation, the chance to beat out the competition in product or process launch, and higher profits. There are also intangible benefits. Employees who have a viable process for using incubation to solve problems will be happier and less stressed. Overall morale can increase as a result and turnover may be reduced. Less tension can also positively affect an employee's health and this may mean fewer sick days and certainly higher productivity. All of these benefits can be the result of the understanding of incubation. This is a small investment for large gains.

Conclusion

There may be great value in bringing the skill of incubation to corporate America. Communication and awareness of the skill will help, as well as the understanding of it and the knowledge to use it. One way to introduce the value of incubation is to incorporate it in training programs. I plan to include incubation training in a professional forum series that I facilitate at my company. I will also spread the word to my management team and to my colleagues in Human Resources. We could also promote the idea to our creativity colleagues, and get their buy-in to bring this skill to their corporate clients. Cultivating ambassadors of this influential skill can help to improve corporate America and help it to build a better, more productive and creative environment, and to be more competitive.

References

Ayan, J. E. (1997). *Aha! 10 ways to free your creative spirit and find your great ideas* (R. Benzel, Ed.). New York, NY: Three Rivers Press.

Bird, B. J. (1989). *Entrepreneurial behavior.* Glenview, IL: Scott, Foresman and Company.

Dacey, J. S., & Lennon, K. H. (1998). *Understanding creativity: The interplay of biological, psychological, and social factors.* San Francisco, CA: Jossey-Bass.

Dodds, R. A., Ward, T. B., & Smith, S. S. (n.d.). *A review of experimental research on incubation in problem solving and creativity.* Retrieved from http://ecologylab.net/research/publications/DoddsSmithWardChapter.pdf

Morris, J. (1992). *Creativity breakthroughs: Tap the power of your unconscious mind.* New York, NY: Warner Books.

Torrance, E. P., & Safter, T. (1990). *The incubation model of teaching: Getting beyond the aha!* Buffalo, NY: Bearly Limited.

Wallas, G. (1931). *The art of thought.* London, England: Jonathan Cape.

Williams, P. (2008, April 29). *What is incubation?* [Web log post]. Retrieved from http://blog.thinkforachange.com/2008/04/29/what-is-incubation.aspx

Appendix A: Interview Results on Incubation

Nine people were interviewed. Questions are listed with the number of responses given. For some questions, more than one answer was permitted.

1. Think about times when you are trying to solve a problem, especially one that uses your creative skills. Did you ever hear the term "incubation?"

8	No
1	Yes

2. How about "sleep on it," "aha," "give it a break?"

9	Yes
0	No

3. Do you purposefully use incubation?

5	No, not deliberately
1	Never thought of using it purposefully
1	Yes, use it often

4. How do you know that you need to incubate or take a break?

5	If I cannot come up with a solution
3	When I become very frustrated
2	If there is no obvious solution
2	After some significant time working on the problem
1	When I fear that the first hunch may result in a bad outcome
1	When my brain is cloudy

5. Can you give me an example of a time when you were working on a problem, took time to incubate, and then came up with the solution? Where were you when the solution came to you?

3	In the car driving
3	Woke up in the middle of the night
3	Having fun
3	During a quiet time
2	In the shower
2	Just before sleep

2	Just waking up
2	Walking
1	While visualizing things
1	While people are talking

6. How do you record your aha moments?

4	Try to remember it
4	Email or text self
3	Leave self voice mail
1	Keep a pad beside the bed and write them down

7. If you knew it would help you come up with a good solution to a problem to purposefully use incubation, would you build it into your process?

9	Yes
0	No

8. Are there any tricks that you use to come up with creative solutions?

4	Collaboration with others to solve the problem
4	Have a mix of people on the team
1	Allow time to actually think of more creative solutions
1	Use magazines or pictures for ideas
1	Technique called "stuffing envelopes" — taking a break and doing a repetitive simple task to let the creative juices flow
1	Allow the group to be silly
1	Throw out a bad idea to spark new ideas

Appendix B: Lesson Plan for Teaching Incubation

Lesson: Learn the skill of incubation in problem solving

Content Goals: Explain incubation
Examine the use of incubation
Discover ways to use the skill in different problem-solving scenarios
Explain the element of the unconscious mind
Explain "aha"

Process Goal:	*Look at it Another Way:* agree to look at problem solving from a different perspective
Materials:	Flip chart paper, markers, Post-it pads, slide deck

Heightening Anticipation

1. Announce to participants that we are going to learn about incubation (*gets them wondering why*).

2. Hand out Post-it notes.

3. Have participants write one thought per Post-it, everything they can think of associated with the word "incubation" (*to help open up their thinking*).

4. After the Post-its are complete, have them pair off and share for five minutes.

5. After they share, ask: "How could the word 'incubation' be associated with problem solving?" (*This introduces the concept that incubation can be associated with problem solving.*)

6. Write down on the flip chart any ideas they have.

Deepening Expectations

1. Ask participants if they have ever "slept on it," "given it a rest," or had an "aha."

2. Teach a lesson about incubation.

   • history

   • details about the discovery of incubation and what it means (time saved, better outcomes, less frustration and negative emotions)

   • uses and triggers for incubation

3. Exercise:

   • Have each participant write down a time when they took a break from a problem. Why did they take a break? (*This relates to the lesson and helps participants to identify their triggers.*)

   • Ask: "What would happen if you took a break sooner?" (*Try to get them to realize that they can build incubation into their process.*)

4. Discuss the concept of using *Look at it Another Way* in regards to the unconscious mind. (*This is weaving an additional creativity skill into the content.*)

- Explain that the concept of the unconscious mind can be foreign and that it will take some active awareness to be able to embrace the concept.

5. Exercise *(fun with the unconscious mind)*:

   - "White" exercise; count the "the's"; young lady/old lady picture

   - Ask: "What does this tell us about our unconscious mind?" (*Gets participants thinking about the fact that their unconscious mind is working.*)

6. Exercise:

   - Have participants write down the last time they had an "aha" when working on a problem at work.

   - Ask: "Where were you and what were you doing?" "What time of day was it?" "How long was it between the time you stopped working on the problem and the time you had the aha?"

Extending the Learning

1. Exercise:

   - Break into groups of four. Ask each group to make a list of ways that they can use incubation the next time they are working on a problem.

   - Have groups report out their lists.

2. Debrief:

   - Ask: "How will these ideas help you to use what you learned today?" "What are some positive results that may occur?"

   - Have participants write down one thing that they will do in the next week to incorporate today's learning.

3. Closing remarks and reminders:

   - Using Incubation is a skill that can save time.

   - The benefits include less frustration, better outcomes.

   - Everyone has one thing they have committed to do in the next week.

   - As with anything, if you don't use it, you won't gain from it.

Part 4:
Creativity in Education

Creativity in Music Education

Jeffrey Glaub

Well, I had done it. I survived my first year of teaching music in a public school, and I finally understood the workplace. I knew the challenges of teaching, the amount of work I would have to finish, the work I would have to do at home, and I was ready to finish the next hurdle to my career: a Master's degree.

To become professionally certified as an educator in New York State, in addition to the four years of undergraduate work, a Master's degree is required. I looked at the requirements, thought about the workload, and started looking at schools. I didn't want to waste my efforts (not to mention my time and money) on a program that wasn't a right fit. So I did the first thing that came to mind: I asked around. What kinds of degrees were others getting?

There was no shortage of opinions. Friends told me about all sorts of programs they were enrolled in, and gave me all kinds of advice and counsel. "Go into administration. You'll make more money!" "Go for music education. You've already got a background." "Go for literacy, everything is about reading now, and you'll be ready if they cut music." And so on. As helpful as everyone was trying to be, there was nothing offered that I hadn't already thought of.

Then came the suggestion that would change my life. I should have realized from my friend's first words that this suggestion—that this program—was different. Every other course of study was presented as a statement: "Take this, because...." Scott O'Dell presented his suggestion in a new way: "Have you considered creativity?"

My first thought was that as a music teacher, creativity was right up my alley. I taught a class that was all about creativity...or so I thought. My concept of creativity was very limited. I thought that creativity in action meant there was a unique product at the end of whatever you did. I was intrigued to see what else I could do to encourage more creativity from my students, especially with the new standards being put in place that would require more testing. Even then, I figured testing must damage the creative output of our students.

I enrolled in my first course in creativity and found that there was more to creativity than making something unique. First, there are the elements of the creative person. I knew some people were more creative than others; how else can you explain the prolific composers like Bach and Schumann writing hundreds of pieces in their lives? But the idea that a person can be creative in different ways was new. For example, we all have strengths in our thinking that fit into certain stages the creative process.

I began by thinking about how this new knowledge could be used to help encourage creativity in my students. I knew that different students learned in different ways, and that to be an effective teacher a variety of teaching strategies would be used. Looking back, I should have realized that different students would have different successes and struggles with creativity.

In addition to the creative person, I learned about the creative process. I had been so focused on what my students were producing that I had neglected the *process* of creating. I began to explore how to better teach my students to go about creating rather than to focus on what they made. I reformed my curriculum and grading by creating several projects that allowed students to worry more about process than product.

My first experiment came near the end of the school year, with my eighth grade students. I provided them very limited instructions, only that they needed to provide for me all the requested information on an assigned composer. Right off the bat, I had several students try to clarify what the parameters were. I had others try to come up with several new ideas for things they could do. Posters, PowerPoints, essays, and verbal reports were all suggested and completed. Some took ideas from previous projects and tried to make them better. Others dove right in and worked the same way they did in the past.

This project changed my view of how my students could use creativity. I saw that students approached creativity differently according to their strengths and preferences. Some students tried to come up with things that were new and things that were unique. One student completely restarted his project when he saw someone else working on something similar. Perhaps most important to me was a simple comment from one of my students. She was an English language learner, someone who did not speak English at the start of the year. She drew a beautiful picture of the composer she had chosen with the facts written around the border of the portrait. When she handed it in, she looked me in the eye and said, "Thank you, Mr. G. You gave me a voice."

That one statement broke me down—I was all in now. I knew from that point forward I needed to make sure that I was allowing my students to be more creative in their learning.

I reformed how I taught my classes and started to incorporate more elements of creativity. My degree put me in a place to teach creativity better and better. I changed my classroom, opening up the floor space to encourage students to change their thinking. I resolved to teach creativity skills to my students. I asked students for input on what to learn and how to perform the songs we sang, and put them into new situations with new challenges. Students were given guidelines for coming up with new ideas and how to select and modify those ideas. I encouraged the notion that no idea was too crazy. For example, one suggestion from the students was, "We should nap in class." We worked out that we couldn't nap in class but we could tame the idea down. Now, we start my class with the older students with a five-minute mediation period. I play reflective music and they take five minutes to consider what is going on in their lives—and it exposes them to classical music, an important part of any music class. It is an example of taking a crazy idea and developing it into a new idea that can work. Students are learning how to use a process to come up with new thinking and how that thinking can be a useful and relevant part of their learning.

That's not to say that there haven't been bumps on the road. I hand in my lesson plans and have often times been asked what these "creativity standards" are. Using these questions as the chance to be an ambassador for creativity, I have explained myself to administrators and other teachers. I tell them: These are the standards that I hold for myself as a teacher in addition to the standards passed down from the state. I find it humorous that they could not put together what the heck this music teacher was doing. "Those aren't Common Core!" "Those aren't music standards, are they?" "What do these creativity standards mean?" I guess the only thing they could see was that there was something odd and extra. They were part right: it was something extra, important and relevant skills that my students need to learn and which would also keep them engaged.

Creative thinking has impacted my own life. My wife and I have been putting together our household and trying to think of new ideas for decoration and set-up. We covered a whole wall with ideas for what to do on our vacations, with an emphasis on coming up with something new. Fairly recently, she told me something that tells me that creativity has changed my private as well as my professional life: "Jeff, *stop facilitating my problem and just listen!*"

To conclude, I say this: *push forward.* Creativity can be a part of every element of your life if you want it to. Find the way to incorporate the wild and crazy. Look for the way to let your dreams be a part of everything you do, and don't be afraid to be different and let new ideas drive you forward.

Integrating Creativity into Science Education

Robin Lee Harris

As I write this I am in the Graduate Certificate program in Creativity and Change Leadership and have one more course before completion. I have been an educational consultant since 1990. In that time I have facilitated many projects and produced many products.

I considered myself to be an effective facilitator before I came to SUNY Buffalo State and learned about the International Center for Studies in Creativity and its program. Now that I know the research, the Creative Problem Solving process, and the skills and strategies, I will be an even better facilitator. The acquisition of creative thinking skills has already changed my teaching! For example, I've already incorporated divergent and convergent thinking tools in my courses. My students, instead of writing a random video reflection after teaching, use the POINt tool—a way to evaluate a concept or idea that begins with the positives of the idea—to write a reflection. They are more thoughtful and suggest more positive changes in their presentations and in their teaching strategies.

On a personal level, my husband and I worked through the CPS process to plan our post-retirement employment. Before learning this process, our discussions went in circles. Now we have a working plan which we are working toward.

In the future, I wish to integrate the principles of CPS, the skills, the tools and attitudes into my teaching of Science Education Methods courses.

After my retirement, what might I do...?

Applied Creativity in Education

David Hoffman

Reviewing the literature on public education these days is often a harsh re-
minder of how many schools are failing our youth in the area of creativity.
Having focused the majority of my graduate degree studies at SUNY Buffalo
State's International Center for Studies in Creativity, I have the advantage to
supplement my teaching skill set with principles of thinking, new models, and
tools that help me to overcome the many challenges educators face in shaping
students into more than just effective test takers.

I have always been of the mind that if I teach students how to learn and think
more effectively, then they will be successful at whatever they face in the future.
Studying creativity has also helped me to become more effective at reaching
students I was not reaching with my old methods; to become more effective
mediating parent concerns; and to create new lessons, units, and tools. Finally,
creativity has inspired me to create new learning models that foster creativity
while remaining within the often-strict guidelines of mandated programs.

In order to help students become more effective and independent thinkers as well
as problem-solvers, I begin the year by weaving in the principles of *convergent*
and *divergent thinking,* as well as utilizing what I call *stem power* in my dialogue
and instructions for activities. I often start the year with warm-ups that call for
students to generate ideas and then prompt them through different challenges
so that the students experience first-hand how these principles improve their
ability to generate ideas and more efficiently narrow and polish these ideas.
Stem power is using sentence stems, phrases such as "Wouldn't it be great if...",
"How might we...", and "How to...?" These encourages students to phrase
problems as solvable opportunities. Combined with divergent thinking, they
learn to generate multiple responses, which helps them overcome the feeling of
always having to provide a "correct" response. Getting students to overcome
this feeling of always having to be right is crucial. The education system and

its increased focus on high-stakes, standardized testing has programmed many students into this mindset, especially by their high school years.

I am constantly utilizing a plethora of other tools I acquired from the creativity field, including a "parking lot" for students to record ideas and thoughts that might not be immediately aligned with the current lesson but might be worth coming back to later. This simple tool and practice gains students' trust and appreciation as they realize the teacher values their ideas. It fosters a culture of open discussion and sharing of experiences that sets up successful discussions on diversity and multiple perspectives when exploring new problems.

In regard to mediating parental concerns, I often find myself using my understanding of assessments such as FourSight and the Myers-Briggs Type Indicator to pay attention to the different personalities involved in the discussion, and how they might differ from my own. This allows me to more effectively assess how to compose myself in a way that will diffuse any possible conflicts in personalities.

I continue to be grateful for having stumbled across the ICSC, and I continue to stay in touch with many of my colleagues in this field and keep abreast of new research, tools, models, and the many ways in which creativity and innovation evolves. As a result of this program, I have become a better teacher. It brings me continued success in creating more independent learners, and I have even begun writing a curriculum to be piloted at the secondary level for a creativity elective.

Helping Universities
Walk the Talk

Maria Macik

"*You study what?*" This is a question I consistently hear when I describe my doctoral program. I am currently in the final stage of my studies...yes, the mountainous dissertation. With hopes of defending within the next year, another item on my expanding "to-do" list has become job searching. I think to myself, "Where should I begin?" Networking and meeting people at professional conferences sounds like a great idea...until that question pops up: "You study what?"

I study creativity. I am fascinated by how people think and how they think creatively. How do we solve problems? How can we help people become better creative thinkers? Not: how can we teach creativity techniques, but rather, how can we truly foster the habits of mind that will increase a person's potential to be creative? With these questions in mind, I have embarked on a journey to find the answers. I am particularly interested in higher education, given that it is the context where we are shaping the minds of our future doctors, engineers, inventors, and so on. Not surprisingly, much of the creativity research has been conducted on either eminent individuals or in the K-12 arena, and little has been done to examine creative learning environments in higher education. There is a lot to learn from these early investigations, however, so it is my goal to use those findings to inform the work in higher education.

Three years ago, I stumbled across a fascinating field: faculty development. As an eager graduate assistant at a center for teaching excellence, I immersed myself in the literature. There is no doubt in my mind that I have found my passion. I love to teach and, even better, I love to inspire others to teach well. I love to listen to people and give advice when it is appropriate. I love helping others, and if I can help someone become a better teacher, then I know I am also impacting the hundreds or thousands of students with whom they interact. Having this new passion made me wonder the ways in which I could use my skills and my understanding of creativity to improve teaching in higher education. Studying the literature, I noticed certain trends and buzzwords. Among them were critical thinking, assessment, reflection, and many more. Often missing from the list was creative thinking. This is where I felt I could fill a void. Clearly, more research needs to be conducted to determine how creative thinking is being fostered in college students. Unfortunately, my degree program is heavily focused on K-12 education, so I am certainly swimming against the tide in my desire to work in higher education. But, is there a creative individual out there who can say that he or she has never had to swim against the tide? It is a common understanding in our field that if you are creative then you tend to challenge the status quo. And so, I choose to challenge both my program and the faculty development field. I choose to challenge my program to demonstrate that creativity can and should be studied in a higher education context. I choose to challenge faculty development to show that creative thinking is a vital skill that college students need. Faculties need more information about creativity, how to foster it, and how to design learning spaces that welcome it.

I encourage you to take a quick glance at the missions and learning outcomes that higher education institutions claim to address. Among those lists, creative thinking or problem solving is usually present. However, in the trenches—in the courses—how is creative thinking embedded? Higher education institutions talk about the importance of fostering innovative thinkers, yet departments or centers for teaching and learning rarely offer programming or resources around the topic of innovation or creativity. Do we expect faculty members to know how to foster this skill? If we indeed hold this expectation, how are we determining whether or not this is actually occurring? Are we examining our degree programs and the learning experiences that our students are engaging in? Are they infused with creativity principles? My sense is that the answers to these questions are not clear. Now is the time to help institutions walk the talk. No longer can we afford to hope that our students will be creative. We must design our classes so that we can foster this skill and increase the potential for its actualization.

When asked the question, "You study what?" I smile and answer, "I study creativity." I help universities walk the talk so that we can ensure that our graduates are creative thinkers and problem solvers. Rather than just helping faculty teach content in better ways, I study creativity so that I can help faculty foster the types of thinking skills that will take disciplinary learning to the next level—the level of synthesizing information, making connections, and solving problems creatively. Rather than feeling that I must follow one path, I know that I can infuse creativity in all that I do. I can help faculty become creative educators, I can help them foster creative thinking in their students, and I can help the faculty development field find creative ways to address the challenges being faced by higher education today. Creativity allows me this type of flexibility. It allows me to not only study it, but, more importantly, to live it.

The Inspire Program

Ted Mallwitz

The Inspire Program is the intersection of my graduate work at the International Center for Studies in Creativity and my work with the Educational Opportunity Program (EOP) at SUNY Buffalo State. EOP combines access, academic support, and supplemental financial assistance to make higher education possible for students who have the potential to succeed, despite poor preparation and limited financial resources. EOP is run on forty-five SUNY campuses. In the quest to find new ways to promote student retention and success, an opportunity presented itself to create a new college success course and program for all 150 freshmen EOP students for the 2013-2014 academic year, which was facilitated through my writing a successful grant proposal for the SUNY Office of Special Programs. After the success of the pilot year of Inspire, the program was renewed for the 2014-2015 academic year and expanded to include an eight-hour introductory workshop as a component of EOP's three-week summer program for freshmen.

The purpose of The Inspire Program is to empower students with the creative problem solving skills, study skills, and strategic planning skills necessary to succeed and achieve at Buffalo State and beyond. The Inspire Creativity & Academic Success course (INS189) focuses on four key areas: creativity, self-reflection, study skills/learning styles, and visionary planning. We believe that every student is creative and possesses the ability to develop the problem solving skills that are essential in their personal, academic, and professional lives. Through the recognition of their creative potential, self-reflection, skill development, and planning for the future, it is our mission to empower students to effectively empower themselves on their paths to academic and life success.

Ten Inspire courses were delivered during the pilot year of the program, led by five instructors, including myself, who are ICSC alumni. These ten classes presented a wonderful opportunity for feedback and refinement. In addition to the courses and the program, we are conducting an impact study on the effects of creativity training on EOP students. The study is now in its second year and has been expanded to include new measures. With the continued support of EOP, this may grow into a longitudinal impact study of creativity training in higher education.

Strengths

This program is mandatory for the EOP freshmen, thus it brings creativity training to a broader population of students at Buffalo State. From the perspective of EOP, there are many college success courses in higher education, but the Inspire Program represents one of the first attempts to approach college success using creative problem solving and creativity training. From the perspective of ICSC, the Inspire Program is a unique application of creativity skills for the deliberate and specific purpose of empowering students to succeed in college.

Potentials

The Inspire Program supports the ICSC's mission to "ignite creativity around the world" by expanding creativity training to more students in the EOP program at Buffalo State. Inspire has been renewed for its second year and we are hopeful that this program will become a permanent part of the freshmen student experience in the EOP program, which would mean that creativity training will effectively be integrated as a lasting component of EOP. The Inspire Program continues to contribute to promoting Creative Studies and the ICSC at Buffalo State. By creating more awareness and interest in Creative Studies through Inspire, it is our hope that more students will choose to enroll in the Creative Studies Undergraduate Minor Program, the Graduate Certificate Program, and even the Master of Science in Creativity.

The accompanying impact study represents the opportunity to contribute new scholarship and research data regarding the effectiveness of creativity training and its ability to improve student performance, resiliency, and retention in higher education. Rather than examining old data, this impact study relies upon the gathering of new and current data on students, which will contribute to creativity scholarship. It is our hope that the Inspire Program impact study will aid in the ICSC's effort to have the CRS205: Introduction to Creativity course become an Intellectual Foundations Course; that is, to mandate creativity training for undergraduate students at Buffalo State.

The Inspire Program also has the potential to extend even further beyond the borders of Buffalo State to other EOP programs in the SUNY system. The Inspire Program can serve the needs of the at-risk student population on a broad scale in both higher education and secondary education.

A Teaching Tune-up

Jeff Olma

This application of creativity—The Teaching Tune-Up Academy—deals with instructional delivery in the classroom. I have used this particular device at the post-secondary level, but I have also presented it for use by teachers of lower grade levels and across all disciplines.

The Teaching Tune-Up Academy uses an array of creative thinking tools to remedy, correct, or strengthen lesson plans for which lesson outcomes are unsatisfactory, an instructor desires to refashion a lesson approach, or an instructor wishes to break away from a method that is no longer productive.

A metaphor that clarifies the experience for teachers is taking one's car in for some kind of corrective service or optimizing work. The "jalopy" of a worn lesson is brought into the Tune-Up session and subjected to performance diagnosis and creative intervention. The desired outcome on a lesson in question is strengthened action, stronger learning outcomes, and enthusiastic faculty ownership.

The lift onto which the problem lesson is hoisted is the Torrance Incubation Model of Teaching and Learning (TIM). In this sense, the mechanics of lesson delivery are first examined in terms of the TIM's three stages: heightening anticipation, deepening expectations, and extending the learning.

Tune-Up sessions are collaborative and emphasize deferring judgment as new approaches are generated and shaped. Participants work in interdisciplinary three person teams. Each teacher chooses a troubled lesson and the team applies the thinking tools to each separate lesson issue.

Each teacher owns his or her own issue or outcome desire. Many creativity tools—Reframing, SCAMPER, Targeting, Evaluation Matrix, ALUo, etc.—can be brought into play. The idea field is richly stretched because of the variety of disciplines that are brought to bear. My job is to facilitate an effective "garage" climate and to employ the tools at all stages of the tune-up. The main deliverable is a freshly shaped lesson and a lesson action plan to help with implementation and desired outcomes.

The reflection piece of the session is a sharing of the original lesson issues, the emergent "re-plan," and the lesson shift(s). Each participant is then encouraged to partner with another teacher and use the partnership to positively assess the results of the re-launched lesson after it has been conducted.

In addition to teaching TIM, the Tune-Up also incorporates aspects of creative thinking, and builds learning and appreciation for creativity in the participants.

In one particular instance, an aviation instructor needed to optimize student learning concerning lift and landing mechanics in aircraft. Rather than rely at first on technical information and jargoned reading, his Tune-Up team suggested a "living-plane" activity in which his inexperienced students "played" at such concepts as traffic control, ailerons and landing gear; then the students were more ready for learning the technical reality of those aspects of aviation. His estimation was that his students took on the concepts through physical learning so that they could better conceptualize and "feel" the mechanics of actual practice.

The Teaching Tune-Up Academy is a dynamic tool for change agency in instructional culture; it brings the power of the Torrance Incubation Model to the instructors' lesson issues; and it fosters personal ownership of ideas and reclaimed instructional creativity.

Teaching for Problem Finding: "Disturbing" How Teachers Teach and "Problematising" How Students Learn

John Yeo

The education system in Singapore is highly regarded as one of the top systems in the world (McKinsey & Co., 2007). Why, then, such a "disturbing" and "problematic" title for this chapter? Some may even argue, if the system isn't broken, why fix it? The fact remains, the education system needs to change in order to stay relevant. In a BBC interview, Singapore's Minister for Education, Heng Swee Keat, said it is "less about content knowledge" and "more about how to process information" (Lim, 2012, para. 3). He described the challenge to innovate as being able to "discern truths from untruths, connect seemingly disparate dots, and create knowledge even as the context changes" (para. 4). What is particularly intriguing to me is the choice of the verbs "discern," "connect," and "create" to describe the dispositions needed to innovate. How do teachers design for learning experiences that draw out such dispositions? How are students able to create new knowledge with the constant change of context if they are unable to pinpoint what exactly might be the right problem to solve? One dimension about teaching for information processing that seems sorely lacking in most curricula is the skill of problem finding.

Teaching for problem finding is a necessary part of creative learning for students. Students today need to acquire problem finding skills as a core competency in order to prepare them to be inventive knowledge workers of the 21st century. Researchers in the field of creativity describe problem finding as an ability to construct, formulate, or otherwise define the problem by retrieval from memory or seeking out new relevant information (Basadur, 1994; Mumford, Mobley, Uhlman, Reiter-Palmon, & Doares, 1991; Runco & Chand, 1994, 1995; Sternberg, 1998; Treffinger, Isaksen, & Dorval, 1994). The distinction often made across the different models of creative problem solving between the initial problem formulation and the other stages highlights that creativity may be more than just problem *solving* (Ward & Kolomyts, 2010). While I have been teaching creative problem solving as pedagogy to encourage more student-centered learning, the reality is that problem finding shouts out as a "null" curriculum. The absence of problem finding in a school's curriculum suggests that teachers are not doing enough to prepare students to search for new problems by themselves, to investigate what a good problem may look like, and to invent new worthwhile problems for their own learning. Wertheimer (cited in Getzels & Csikszentmihalyi, 2007) puts it best:

> [T]he function of thinking is not just solving an actual problem but discovering, envisaging, going deeper into questions. Often in great discoveries the most important thing is that a certain question is found. Envisaging, putting the productive question, is often a more important, often a greater achievement than the solution of a set of questions. (p. 103)

From a teaching and learning perspective, this opens up promising avenues of inquiry that may lead to deeper insight in any subject discipline.

Runco (1994) is of the opinion that problem finding can be seen as a reaction against the application of traditional problem solving ideas to creativity. Most researchers in creativity hold the view that traditional problem solving is "inadequate to explain how creators come to realize that a problem exists in the first place, and how they are motivated to proactively bring their subjective experience to understand the problem" (Kozebelt, Beghetto, & Runco, 2010). The purpose of this article is to stir a sense of wonderment that provokes you to ask, "What might teachers do to teach for problem finding skills?" Some teachers may see the use of problem-based learning and project-based learning as approaches to teach for problem solving skills across the different subject disciplines, but these pedagogies are insufficient to help students sharpen their ability to problem find.

Problems with Singapore Teachers' Conception of Creativity and Problem Finding

The teaching of creativity within the curriculum as it currently stands is "highly contentious (even) amongst creativity theorists and stems from how researchers and scholars conceptualize creativity" (Yeo, 2011, p. 37). One reason for this challenge could be the fact that there is a greater emphasis placed on the broad spectrum of *critical* thinking skills, as compared to *creative* thinking skills, with the latter being much less tested. Hence, teachers are less motivated to understand what creative thinking is and to deliberate on how students can better acquire creative thinking skills. A secondary analysis of Singapore students' 2009 Program for International Student Assessment (PISA) performance reveals Singapore students are ranked relatively low in their creativity and meta-cognitive skills as compared to other top performing systems. This further suggests that the teaching of thinking skills and meta-cognition may be uneven across the system and is not consistently taught with the same level of effectiveness by teachers. Based on the experience of working across different schools, I suspect there is a fundamental problem that has seldom been addressed: many teachers perceive that effective thinking is *all* about skills.

The above problem is part of my findings in a pre-course survey that I implemented with Singapore school middle managers attending my class on Applied Creative Problem Solving. With the survey question "What roles do schools play in nurturing creativity in our students?", 92% of the participants (168 respondents from July 2009 to January 2012) listed different types of thinking skills, strategies and programs in schools used to develop students' creativity. With that same question, 76% described creativity being taught or infused in curriculum either through subject-disciplines, project work, competitions, or other co-curricular activities. Of the 168 participants, only two noted that the ability to teach creatively—one of the core competencies under cultivating knowledge—is part of the Teacher Competency Model that has been disseminated to all schools since 2005 (see the figure below).

Core Competency
• Nurturing The Whole Child

Cultivating Knowledge
• Subject Mastery
• Analytical Thinking
• Initiative
• Teaching Creatively

Winning Hearts & Minds
• Understanding the Environment
• Developing Others

Working With Others
• Partnering Parents
• Working in Teams

Knowing Self & Others
• Tuning into Self
• Personal Integrity
• Understanding Others
• Respecting Others

Teaching Competency Model (Source: Singapore Ministry of Education, 2005)

In addition, although 87% of respondents claimed they are teaching creative thinking, when asked to provide concrete examples only 21% provided details on how their teaching leads to evidence of measurement of students' creative achievements. Many point to the use of assessment rubrics to evaluate students' creative products. However, I (Yeo, 2011) make the distinction that

> the complexities of evaluating the creative process in tandem with assessing the final product may not be as easy. Teachers acknowledge the challenge of designing an engaging and effective facilitation process and research also informs that such instructive roles of teachers need to be carefully reconsidered to better support students' creative functioning. Teachers work hard to help students fulfill the standards for descriptors pertaining to students' ideas, such as "insightful and/or innovative," "well-supported," "thoroughly analyzed and evaluated," and "organized coherently." (p. 41)

Few teachers realize that creativity is not only taught but also needs to be "caught," with teachers themselves actively modeling creative learning. How might schools as an ecosystem of learning be better able to create a culture that gets both teachers and students to think creatively together? Besides these concerns, my research (Yeo, 2011) also shows that teachers on the ground face many other challenges in facilitating for creative thinking often without any support or resources.

While the above findings already pose a big challenge in pushing ahead for a more creative curriculum, the path to helping teachers understand the importance of problem finding is even more daunting. The reason is quite obvious: again, there is little empirical research such as meta-analytic studies done to confirm the educative value of problem-finding as a curriculum agenda. The few research studies that have been done suggest that problem finding is more subjective-oriented than problem solving, as the precise nature of problem finding is still very much unclear (Csikszentmihalyi & Getzels, 1989; Dudek & Cote, 1994; Kozbelt, 2008; Moore, 1985; Runco, 1994).

Situating Problem-finding in the Curriculum

We are already living *in* the 21st century. Popular frameworks proposed for 21st century teaching and learning (such as Partnership for 21st Century Skills, 2007; NCREL, 2003; Trilling & Fadel, 2009) highlight problem solving as a core competency. A closer examination shows none of these frameworks posits the need for students to acquire the skill to become effective problem finders. Interestingly, these frameworks were conceptualized at a time when industry feedback remarked on the absence of risk-taking and entrepreneurial dispositions (Trilling & Fadel, 2009). Across these frameworks, they identified problem solving that deals particularly with solving non-familiar and unconventional problems (Buck Institute for Education [BIE], 2008). How then does the curriculum support this way of dealing with unfamiliar and unconventional problems? How would our current mode of teaching help students to develop cognitive schemas based on defining factors or attributes of a problem before they are able to deepen their understanding of content?

The Singapore Ministry of Education (MOE, 2010) conceptualized Curriculum 2015 (C2015) that enumerates a set of broad student learning outcomes centered on 21st century skills and competencies. The C2015 learning outcomes feature the domain of critical and inventive thinking skills (see Appendix), proposing the need for students to have a sense of curiosity and creativity by having a "desire to seek and learn new knowledge." However, these learning outcomes do not mention explicitly how or why problem finding needs to be considered as part of the core competencies. Much research has showed that children are naturally curious; teaching problem finding ought to build on such a student-centric disposition. Teachers recognize the need to cultivate curiosity and creativity in students but many lack the knowledge and skills to arouse students' curiosity for learning and sustaining students' playfulness, and to look for different ways of learning. Are teachers really ill-prepared to support such forms of creative learning whereby students learn to discover problems or reframe issues to identify critical aspects for problem solving? Kapur (National Institute of Education [NIE], 2012, p. 8) suggests that there is a gap in our understanding of problem finding as a process, particularly in the practice of math in schools as the mathematical problem "is either fully specified or known to a great degree." In addition, he opined that having good problem solving skills may have little relationship to the level of one's problem finding skills. He elaborates that there is an assumption that "students have sufficient knowledge to solve problems because they have been taught and the goal is specified." However in problem finding, he suggests that "we may not even have enough knowledge to solve the problem, which is the case in many of the challenges we encounter in life" (p. 7).

Conclusion: Problems Finding the Problem

Albert Einstein once said that problem formulation is more important than its solution since "to raise new questions, new possibilities, to regard old questions from a new angle, requires creative imagination and marks real advance" (Einstein & Infeld, 1938/1971). While curriculum documents have been carefully planned and neatly culminate into teaching syllabus that delineate well-categorized learning objectives, does the delivery of these "neatly structured" teaching materials constrain the creative learning space for students to enjoy free imagination and explore radically different problems that interest them?

In the earlier mentioned survey I implemented for MLS participants in my elective, the two most often cited challenges for a creative education are high-stakes testing and lack of curriculum time. While we have no magic bullet for these challenges, nonetheless, it leaves me to wonder how should teachers reduce the over-teaching that arises out of anxiety over exam preparation that is so often blamed for "squeezing out" the creativity in education? Would the teaching for problem finding help to bring about greater spontaneity and new ways of demonstrating personal creativity that celebrate individual achievements across different domains and aspects of schooling? Even with the absence of problem finding, will the Singapore MOE's 21st Century Competency framework featuring the Critical and Inventive Thinking standards and benchmarks (see Appendix) result only in an outcomes-based approach?

With students as top of mind, preparing them with the skill of problem finding may radically deepen their sense of creativity. It may also change the way teachers regard the necessary shift to co-create knowledge with students' self-constructed problems. Many educational researchers and practitioners have written that there is adequate empirical evidence of problem solving as a type of metacognitive process that enhances learning effectiveness (Brown, 1978, 1987; Desoete, 2007; Fisher, 1998). Granted that such forms of learning will create new levels of "discomfort"—for both teachers and students—then a question to ask would be what purpose does problem finding serve in the curriculum? If problem finding is really able to heighten students' sense of wonderment and curiosity, then there is a need to more closely examine what it takes to support teachers' capabilities to design a more generative and explorative way of looking at problems.

References

Basadur, M. (1994). Managing the creative process in organizations. In M. A. Runco (Ed.), *Problem finding, problem solving, and creativity.* (pp. 237-268). Norwood, NJ: Ablex Publishing Company.

Brown, A. (1987). Metacognition, executive control, self-regulation, and other more mysterious mechanisms. In F. E. Weinert & R. H. Klue (Eds.), *Metacognition, motivation and understanding* (p. 65-116). Hillsdale, NJ: Lawrence Erlbaum.

Brown, A. L. (1978). Knowing when, where and how to remember: A problem of metacognition. In R. Glaser (Ed.), *Advances in instructional psychology*, Vol. 1 (pp. 77-165). Hillsdale, NJ: Lawrence Erlbaum Associates.

Buck Institute for Education (2008). *BIE 21st century skills table.* Retrieved from http://www.bie.org/research/21st_century_skills

Csikszentmihalyi, M. & Getzels, J. W. (1989). Creativity and problem finding. In F. H. Farley & R. W. Neperud (Eds.), *The foundations of aesthetics* (pp. 91-116). New York, NY: Praeger.

Desoete, A. (2007). Improving the mathematics teaching-learning process through metacognition. *Electronic Journal of Research in Educational Psychology, 5,* 705-730.

Dudek, S. Z., & Cote, R. (1994). Problem finding revisited. In M. A. Runco (Ed.), *Problem finding, problem solving, and creativity* (pp. 130-150). Norwood, NJ: Ablex.

Einstein, A., & Infeld, L. (1971). *The evolution of physics: From early concepts to relativity and quanta.* Cambridge, England: Cambridge University Press. (Original work published 1938)

Fisher, R. (1998). Thinking about thinking: Developing metacognition in children. *Early Child Development and Care, 141,* 1-13.

Getzels, J. W., & Csikszentmihalyi, M. (2007). From problem solving to problem finding. In I. A. Taylor & J. W. Getzels (Eds.), *Perspectives in creativity* (pp. 90-116). Piscataway, NJ: AldineTransaction.

Kozbelt, A. (2008). Hierarchical linear modeling of creative artists' problem solving behaviors. *Journal of Creative Behavior, 42,* 181-200.

Kozebelt, A., Beghetto, R. A., & Runco, M. A. (2010). Theories of creativity. In J. C. Kaufman & R. J. Sternberg (Eds.), *The Cambridge handbook of Creativity* (pp. 20-47). New York, NY: Cambridge University Press.

Lim, R. (22 May, 2012). Singapore wants creativity not cramming. *BBC News Business.* Retrieved from http://www.bbc.co.uk/news/business-17891211

McKinsey & Co. (2007, September). *How the world's best-performing school systems come out top.* Retrieved in 2007 from http://www.mckinsey.com/App_Media/Reports/SSO/Worlds_School_Systems_Final.pdf

Ministry of Education (2005). *Enhanced Performance Management System.* Singapore: Ministry of Education.

Ministry of Education (2010, March). *Nurturing our young for the future: Competencies for the 21st century.* Retrieved from http://www.moe.edu.sg

Moore, M. (1985). The relationship between the originality of essays and variables in the problem-discovery process: A study of creative and non-creative middle school students. *Research in the Teaching of English, 19,* 84-95.

Mumford, M. D., Mobley, M. I., Uhlman, C. E., Reiter-Palmon, R., & Doares, L. M. (1991). Process analytic models of creative thought. *Creativity Research Journal, 4,* 91-122.

National Institute of Education (2012, July/August). *SingTeach.* Retrieved from http://singteach.nie.edu.sg/wp-content/uploads/SingTeach_Issue37.pdf

NCREL (2003). *EnGauge 21st Century Skills: Literacy in the Digital age.* Retrieved from http://www.ncrel.org/engauge/skills/skills.htm

Partnership for 21st Century Skills (2007). *The intellectual and policy foundations of the 21st century skills framework.* Tucson, AZ: Partnership for 21st Century Skills.

Runco, M. A., & Chand, I. (1994). Conclusions concerning problem finding, problem solving, and creativity. In M. A. Runco (Ed.), *Problem finding, problem solving, and creativity* (pp. 217-290). Norwood, NJ: Ablex Publishing Company.

Runco, M. A., & Chand, I. (1995). Cognition and creativity. *Education Psychology Review, 7,* 243-267.

Runco, M. A. (Ed.). (1994). *Problem finding, problem solving, and creativity.* Norwood, NJ: Ablex Publishing Company.

Sternberg, R. J. (1998). A three-facet model of creativity. In R. J. Sternberg (Ed.), *The nature of creativity: Contemporary psychological perspectives* (pp. 125-147). Cambridge, UK: Cambridge University Press.

Torrance, E. P. (1979). *The search for satori and creativity.* Buffalo, NY: Creative Education Foundation.

Treffinger, D. J., Isaksen, S. G., & Dorval, K. B. (1994). Creative problem solving: An overview. In M. A. Runco (Ed.), *Problem finding, problem solving, and creativity* (pp. 223-236). Norwood, NJ: Ablex Publishing Company.

Trilling, B. & Fadel, C. (2009). *21st century skills: Learning for life in our times.* San Francisco, CA: Jossey-Bass.

Ward, B. T. & Kolomyts, Y. (2010). Cognition and creativity. In J. C. Kaufman & R. J. Sternberg (Eds.), *The Cambridge handbook of creativity* (pp. 93-112). New York, NY: Cambridge University Press.

Yeo, J. (2011). Authentic assessment for creativity as a 21st century pedagogy. In K. H. Koh & J. Yeo (Eds.), *Mastering the art of authentic assessments: From challenges to champions* (pp. 37-54). Singapore: Pearson Education South Asia.

Appendix

Standards and Benchmarks for Critical and Inventive Thinking Skills in Curriculum 2015 Framework

Sound Reasoning and Decision-Making refers to the development of well-constructed explanations and well-substantiated conclusions through analysis, comparison, inference/interpretation, evaluation and synthesis of evidence and arguments. Sound Reasoning and Decision-Making includes:

- extracting implications and conclusions from facts, premises, ethical issues, or data;

- constructing relationships between the essential elements of a problem;

- challenging social norms to provide alternative theories and explanation.

Reflective Thinking refers to the questioning and refining of thoughts, attitudes, behavior and actions. Reflective Thinking includes:

- suspending judgment;

- reassessing conclusions and considering alternatives;

- stepping back to take the larger picture into account.

Curiosity and Creativity refers to the desire to seek and learn new knowledge; and generate relatively novel and appropriate ideas or new products. Curiosity and Creativity includes:

- being resourceful, flexible and adaptable;

- willing to take risks and accept mistakes;

- having the ability to envisage possible futures.

Managing Complexities and Ambiguities refers to the modification of thinking, attitudes, behavior and/or skills to adapt to diverse demands and challenges in new, unfamiliar contexts. Managing Complexities and Ambiguities includes:

- tolerating ambiguity;

- considering and accepting alternative perspectives, solutions or methods;

- taking on diverse roles;

- multi-tasking;

- being resilient and focused on pursuing goals despite difficulties and unexpected complications.

LEARNING OUTCOME:

Generates novel ideas; exercises sound reasoning and reflective thinking to make good decisions; and manages complexities and ambiguities

Standards		Benchmarks			
	By End of Primary 3	By End of Primary 6	By End of Secondary 2	By End of Secondary 4/5	By End of Junior College 2 / Pre-University 3
CIT 1 Explores possibilities and generates ideas	1.1a The student is able to generate ideas to respond to an issue/challenge.	1.1b The student is able to generate ideas and explore different pathways to respond to an issue/challenge.	1.1c The student is able to generate ideas and explore different pathways that are appropriate for responding to an issue/challenge.	1.1d The student is able to generate ideas and explore different pathways that lead to solutions.	
CIT 2 Exercises sound reasoning and decision making	2.1a The student is able to explain his/her reasoning and decisions.	2.1b The student is able to use evidence to explain his/her reasoning and decisions.	2.1c The student is able to use evidence and adopt different viewpoints to explain his/her reasoning and decisions.	2.1d The student is able to use evidence and adopt different viewpoints to explain his/her reasoning and decisions, having considered the implications of the relationship among different viewpoints.	
	2.2a The student is able to recount relevant experiences which he/she has learnt from.	2.2b The student is able to reflect on his/her thoughts, attitudes, behavior and actions during the learning experiences and determine the modifications required.		2.2d The student is able to suspend judgment, reasses conclusions and consider alternatives to refine his/her thoughts, attitudes, behavior and actions.	
CIT 3 Manages complexities and ambiguities	3.1a The student is able to identify the expectations of the task/role and stay focused on them.	3.1b The student is able to identify essential elements of multiple tasks/roles, stay focused on them and persevere when he/she encounters difficulties and unexpected challenges.		3.1d The student is able to identify essential elements of complex tasks, stay focused on them, take on diverse roles and persevere when they encounter difficulties and unexpected challenges.	
		3.2b The student is able to accept different perspectives, solutions and/or methods, even in the face of uncertainty.		3.2d The student is able to manage uncertainty and adapt to diverse demands and challenges.	

Investigating Functional Fixedness in Student-Designed Survival Kits

Suzanna J. Ramos

Picture this: Fifteen student projects on survival kits all looking alike. The projects are of various sizes, shapes and colors, but they still resemble first aid kits. I scratch my head and look at my grading rubrics. I ponder. *Didn't I include points for creativity?*

That was almost ten years ago. Before pursuing my Master's degree in Creativity, I felt I was a creative geography teacher. For example, for my lesson on natural disasters, instead of simply going through all the hard facts about the dangers of floods, I got my students to design a survival kit for such a disaster. However, despite brainstorming for ideas, nearly all my students produced some type of box to house medicine and food items. Others produced various floating devices or boat-like structures.

After my 15-month sojourn at the International Center for Studies in Creativity, I was armed with literature on creativity. One aspect of creativity that caught my attention was the phenomenon of functional fixedness (Smith, Ward, & Schumacher, 1993). In their study, participants were asked to generate designs for as many toys or imaginary creatures as they could for twenty minutes. One group was given examples ("fixation" condition) but was told not to follow those examples. Another group of participants was not shown any examples at all (control condition). The results showed that the latter group was more likely to generate more creative ideas that did not include some features from the examples. Further, Ward's (1995) model of the "path of least resistance" states that when people develop new ideas for a certain domain, the tendency is to use basic exemplars with which they are familiar in the domain and use those examples as a starting point.

Currently as a Ph.D. student, I constantly reflect on my teaching experiences and ask myself how my teaching pedagogy could be improved when I learn a new concept in creativity. For instance, I considered what I might learn from the survival kit lesson. I had shown the students visual examples of what kits looked like and specifically instructed them not to produce box-like kits. It frustrated me at the time, but now it made sense: My students experienced functional fixedness when it came to designing their projects, which prevented them from producing more original designs.

I decide to explore this phenomenon to see if there was a way of removing functional fixedness when designing an innovative product. The goal is to achieve an ideal final result—the best possible creative and original product (Altshuller, 1996). In this particular instance, the final product would not even resemble common conceptions of what a survival kit looked like.

My Humble Quest

Fifty-five undergraduates from Texas A&M University volunteered to participate in an exploratory study. All were enrolled in the Creative Studies minor course Creativity and Creative Problem Solving (EPSY 432). These students had taken at least one other Creative Studies Minor course in the previous semester, so they were adequately familiar with creativity, especially Creative Problem Solving (CPS).

The students were divided into two groups. Group A consisted of 33 students. For this group, I had a 10-minute discussion on what constituted a survival kit. I collected responses such as "it normally has a handle," "it is a container to carry items around," "it has zippers." Appendix A provides a complete list of these responses. I wrote their responses on the whiteboard and crossed out each response with a red marker, instructing them NOT to include any of those features in their drawings—a condition known as the "Ideal Final Result" (IFR) found in Appendix B. The students' task was to draw the front and side views, as well as label the parts they felt were important. They had 20 minutes to complete the task.

Group B consisted of 22 students. They were located in a different room with another experimenter, also a student with a Master's degree in Creativity. The participants were asked to draw a survival kit to be used in times of a flood. There was no discussion about the requirements of the survival kit or an IFR condition. Participants were simply told to draw the front and side views, as well as label the parts they felt were important. They, too, were given 20 minutes to complete the task.

Three other graduate students with a background in creativity studies rated all the drawings. They each received Appendix A (student responses of what a survival kit looks like) and told that a drawing was deemed to be creative if it did not contain any of those features. The raters were given a sheet of paper with the words "Creative" and "Not Creative" and were instructed to check the appropriate box for each drawing. They were also told not to discuss with the other raters, but if a rater was unsure, there needed to be a final consensus amongst the three raters. However, this situation did not arise. After the completion of the rating process, there was 100% inter-rater reliability.

Results

The breakdown of the results is presented in Table 1. For Group A, participants were asked to provide their own responses on what a kit looked like, but given specific instructions not to base their drawings on those responses. Only 51.6% yielded creative survival kits. Although many of the student-generated kit characteristics were absent in their drawings (e.g., presence of handles, box-like, presence of zippers), 48.4% of the drawings were deemed uncreative because they were containers of some kind with a flotation device. All of these contained items that were necessary for survival like food, drink, medicine, and other items like flashlight and switchblade. This was in direct violation of the IFR, where students were instructed not to draw containers or receptacles of any sort.

Table 1. *Creativity ratings for student-designed survival kits*

Group	Number of Participants	Learning Condition	% Creative	% Not Creative
A	33	IFR discussed	51.6	48.4
B	22	IFR not discussed	13.7	86.3

Drawings that were considered creative followed the IFR and did not have most or all of the student-generated list of kit features. Two examples from Group A that were considered creative are provided in Figure 1. In these drawings, the students did not concentrate on the items that could be found in a survival kit. Instead, they explored ways on how to survive in a flood. The use of a survival ball and inflatable shoes are creative ways to survive during a flood. These drawings and others in this group did not exhibit typical features of a kit and were close to the IFR condition. Two examples from the same group that were not considered creative are provided in Figure 2. Although they did not resemble typical survival kits in that they did not have handles or were box-like, they still represented containers of some sort to keep items that were considered necessary for survival. More than 95% of the students from this group drew containers that were creative in nature but they still held implicit conceptions of a typical kit. This was so despite the fact that they were explicitly told not to draw survival kits that were container-like in nature.

For Group B, 86.3% of the drawings were deemed uncreative. This was the group where they were told to draw a survival kit in times of a flood with no

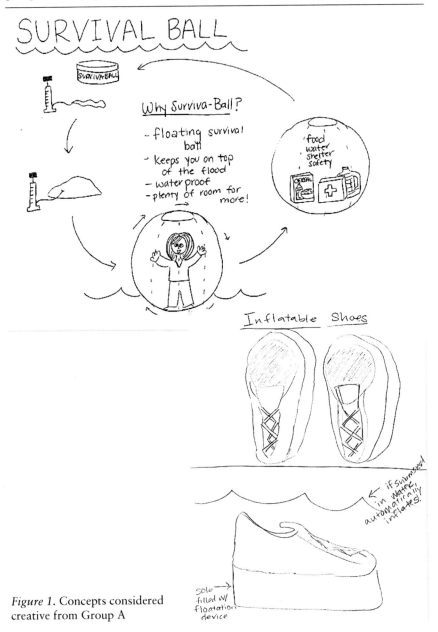

Figure 1. Concepts considered creative from Group A

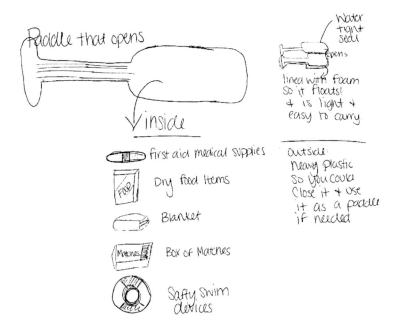

Paddle that opens

Water tight seal
opens
lined with foam so it floats! & is light & easy to carry.

↓ inside

first aid medical supplies

Dry food Items

Blanket

Box of Matches

Safty swim devices

Outside:
heavy plastic so you could close it & use it as a paddle if needed

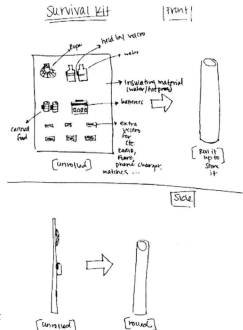

Survival kit | Front |

rope
held by velcro
water
→ Insulating material (water/fire prot)
→ batteries
→ extra scisors for etc: Radio, Flare, phone charger, matches...
canned food

[unrolled]

[Roll it up to store it]

| Side |

[unrolled] [rolled]

Figure 2. Concepts considered not creative from Group A

other accompanying instructions. Although this group had experience with creativity tools for idea generation, a large proportion of their drawings were not considered creative by the raters. 95% of the drawings were containers of some sort to hold survival items together in one place. One example is given in Figure 3.

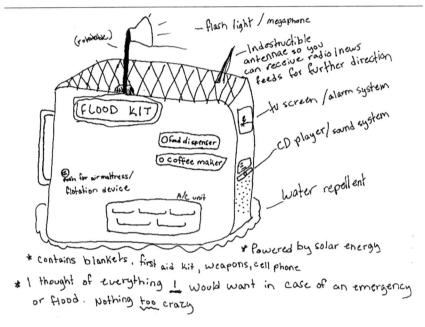

Figure 3. Concept considered not creative from Group B

Just in case you missed it, notice that this student wrote "nothing too crazy" on the diagram! Although the students were taught to defer judgment when producing ideas for a project or assignment during their coursework, this fundamental principle of divergent thinking was cast aside.

A mere 13.7% of the students' drawings were rated creative in this second group. In this case, although there were some items kept in the survival kit, it was not in the form of a typical container. An example is provided in Figure 4.

Considering that this is a group of students who had studied at least one Creativity minor course and are currently undergoing a course on CPS, the students did not utilize the tools they had learned in designing and drawing a creative survival kit that was atypical. Their fixedness with the term "kit" possibly caused them to think of a box-like structure with survival equipment.

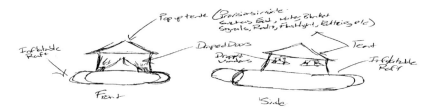

Figure 4. Concept considered creative from Group B

Discussion

As a professional in the field of creative thinking I have realized the significant role of functional fixedness in teaching students to behave creatively when given a challenging task. Before the study, I had expected that students who studied creativity would produce more original designs, and that a high percentage of the drawings would not contain features of a typical kit. My assumption is that students who have gone through a course on creative thinking will be able to use the tools they had learned in generating creative ideas and products. However, the results did not conclusively highlight this finding. One possibility is that functional fixedness is still strong in the minds of the students and the word "kit" still connotes a receptacle that houses important items for survival. The creative drawings verged more on how one can survive during the flood itself rather than how to sustain your life during or after a flood. Despite the instructions by the experimenter to not depend on their common conceptions of what a survival kit looked like, a large proportion of the students still had those features in their drawings.

Functional fixedness may have been caused by the students' desire to get the "right answer," and therefore shy away from anything original. This means that past experience (what they have seen) has more influence than imagination (what they have not seen). This desire to get the right answer also leads to a strict interpretation of the word "kit" (what it is) instead of a flexible interpretation (what it could be given a desired function). Students therefore start thinking more in concrete terms around objects instead of abstract terms around functions.

There could also be a time factor challenge. Since the students had only twenty minutes to design, they may unconsciously believe it is a sort of exam or at least have the impression that there is no time to think about it and start drawing the first thing that comes to their minds. Since one's acquired knowledge (past experience) is generally the first thing that we call to mind, it has priority over engaging the imagination. I wonder whether the same students could produce more novel designs if they were given a week to produce them. Would they, for instance, have questioned the word "kit?" Would they have used more of their acquired CPS skills?

Further, 90% of the designs had some sort of flotation device, thus giving weight to Ward's (1995) model of the "path of least resistance." This model states that when people develop new ideas for a certain domain, the tendency is to use basic exemplars that they are familiar with in the domain and use those examples as a starting point. Indeed, one basic exemplar, flotation, was on the minds of the students when they thought about surviving a flood. Or perhaps the word "kit" conjured up images of the kit as a static physical product, rather than a functional product that helps one to survive a flood.

This exploratory study has implications for teaching and instruction. Students are expected to generate creative ideas for projects and assignments. However, implicit fixedness can detract them from producing original ideas. In my case, I assumed that simply providing students with tools and techniques of creativity can help my students generate original ideas.

I have come away with a few learning points as a result of this simple study. First, I learned that I need to be aware of the kind of instructions I provide or the teaching process I use to help students to produce novel and useful ideas. I may be able to get students to use the creativity tools correctly, but I also need to be aware that certain words or jargon can produce fixedness in my students' implicit thinking. In this case, a simple word like "kit" can elicit images that prevent my students from looking beyond those images.

Second, if I had the opportunity to conduct this lesson again, I would take some time to teach students about functional fixedness and how it happens. Their awareness could lead them to question those traits or characteristics of objects that we take for granted and think more in terms of functions to answer the question, "What do I want the object (kit) to do for me?" (Bettencourt & Ulwick, 2008).

Third, I would spend more time discussing what a survival kit might look like with my students. They could be in cooperative learning groups to discuss their responses. Using their peers' feedback, the students could produce their drawings, improve on them and then draw another design. I would get them to explain how they would tweak the drawing such that they will be able to get to the best ideal final result.

References

Altshuller, G. (1996). *And suddenly the inventor appeared: TRIZ, the theory of inventive problem solving.* Worcester, MA: Technical Innovation Center, Inc.

Bettencourt, L. A., & Ulwick, A. W. (2008). The customer-centered innovation map. *Harvard Business Review, 86*(5), 109-114.

Smith, S. M., Ward, T. B., & Schumacher, J. S. (1993). Constraining effects of examples in a creative generation task. *Memory and Cognition, 21*(6), 837-845.

Ward, T. B. (1995). What's old about new ideas? In S. M. Smith, T. B. Ward, & R. A. Finke (Eds.), *The creative cognition approach* (pp. 157-178). Cambridge, MA: MIT Press.

Appendix A

List of student-generated responses on how a survival kit in times of a flood will typically look like:

- It normally has a handle.
- It is a container to carry items around.
- It has a zipper.
- It has pockets.

Appendix B

Ideal Final Result (your survival kit must not have the following features):

- Must not have a handle.
- Must not resemble a container of some sort.
- Must not have a zipper.
- Must not have pockets.

Part 5:
Applications of Creativity

What Does Creative Leadership Look Like in a Crisis Situation?

Alison L. Murphy

The Idle Tuesday (or Thursday, For That Matter)

Baz Luhrmann's famous "Sunscreen"[1] played through my head after hanging up the phone with the police department one sunny Thursday in October: "the real troubles in your life are apt to be things that never crossed your worried mind, the kind that blindside you at 4 p.m. on some idle Tuesday." My family had been summoned to the police department in a little town an hour's drive away, where, in a cramped basement conference room, we were questioned for over three hours.

"Weren't those officers lovely?" my 84-year-old mother asked as we made our way to the car in a stunned stupor. She wasn't concerned by the incessant questioning of the "nice officers" who collected our birth dates, social security and driver's license numbers before determining we had no role in a federal extortion crime. Pulling away from the station, it was apparent an idle Tuesday had arrived.

Meet the Flintstones

J. and M. Flintstone,[2] my 93 and 94 year old aunt and uncle, have seemingly been around forever. They live alone, chose not to have children, worked all their lives and are very private people. Sadly, they were systematically robbed of

---

1   http://www.youtube.com/watch?v=sTJ7AzBIJoI. There is debate regarding whether or not Mr. Luhrmann actually wrote this song and whether or not it's actually a song or a commencement speech, or both.
2   Names are changed to protect the innocent.

approximately a million dollars over six years. None of us really knew they: 1) had lost their cognitive abilities, much less suffered from dementia; 2) had any real money (we felt guilty cashing the $25 checks they sent for our birthdays); and 3) had been befriended by two different sets of thieves.

About that third item: in M's words, "we were helping a young couple just getting started." J's friend—Big Jimmy—"just needed a bit of help now and then." (J couldn't remember how he met Big Jimmy or why Jimmy needed help.) My uncle was an accountant. He kept detailed records each time the young couple and the friend "borrowed" money; making them sign a promissory note for a payback with interest.[3] When we arrived from the police station, we found their house stuffed with hundreds of piles of paper, old bills, junk mail, newspapers, coupons, grocery receipts, unfiled tax returns, and most importantly, little yellow sheets of legal paper, thousands of little yellow slips, all neatly listing the amount borrowed, the reason for the "loan," and a signature, promising a payback. He couldn't remember the last time he had eaten but he knew, down to the penny, how much money he had "loaned."

They Sunk My Boat–or, Are Leaders Born or Made?

When asked how he became a leader, President John F. Kennedy is reported to have said, "It was easy; someone sunk my boat," referring to how he took a leadership role when his PT-109 boat was sunk in the South Pacific during World War II.[4] This brings to mind the proverbial question, are leaders born or made?

According to Northhouse (2010, p. 1), "Some researchers conceptualize leadership as a trait, or as a behavior, whereas others view leadership from an information-processing perspective or relational standpoint." Northhouse asserts there are two primary views of leadership: *assigned leadership* (resulting from an individual's assigned position within an organization or structure), and *emergent leadership* (those that others perceive as the most influential member of a group or organization, regardless of the individual's title). The emergent view of leadership dovetails with what Northhouse calls the *situational approach* to leadership: "As the name implies, situational leadership focuses on leadership in situations. The premise of the theory is different situations demand different kinds of leadership" (p. 89).

Situational leadership (Northhouse, 2010) is a prescriptive approach to leadership that suggests how leaders can become effective in many different types of organizational settings involving a wide variety of organizational tasks. The approach provides a model that suggests to leaders how they should behave based

---

3   To put this in perspective, J and M withdrew from their bank amounts ranging from $300 to $9,800 two to three times a week. The nice young couple and Big Jimmy would wait in the bank parking lot for J to come out with the cash.

4   http://www.historynet.com/pt-109-disaster.htm

on the demands of a particular situation" (p. 107). Situational leadership—say, having your boat sunk on an idle Tuesday—plays well with Mumford, Zaccaro, Harding, Jacobs, and Fleishman's (2000) assertion that leadership is complex and leadership problems differ from more routine problems because they are more complex, include conflict, and are ill-defined:

> Still another way leadership problems differ from more routine kinds of problems is that they tend to be novel. Many routine managerial problems, business projections for example, do not represent especially novel problems to experienced managers (Nutt, 1984). These routine organization issues do not call for exceptional leadership. Leadership, however, becomes more crucial when one must develop and guide adaptive responses to new or changing situations. (p. 14)

I think it is fair to say the Flintstone case clearly meets the definition provided by Mumford et al. (2000) of a "problem," reinforced by Puccio, Mance, and Murdock (2011), that "the types of problems leaders face are ill-defined (i.e., no single solution path), novel (i.e., the situation is either changing or new), and complex (i.e., information is missing or it is difficult to determine what is relevant" (p. 44). Further, the Flintstones possessed a heuristic problem, representing both a predicament and an opportunity. In other words, they had an open-ended challenge with no set method to follow or obvious solution available (Puccio et al., 2011, p. 36). To put it mildly, they had a "difficult, complicated, or perplexing situation for which a new approach must be devised to return to current levels of performance" (Puccio et al., 2011, p. 36). Proactive problem-solving is described by Puccio et al. (2011) as "the pursuit of a vision or establishing goals" (p. 35).

But, what happens when the vision is completely unclear, and in the case of my aunt and uncle, the predicament is potentially life threatening? How can a newly-appointed situational leader (read: me) successfully use deliberate creativity to first stabilize and, second, improve the outcome of the situation?

Clarifying the Problem

When discussing the Creative Problem Solving (CPS) process, Osborn (1953/2001) stressed the importance of finding a problem to be solved: "Sometimes we must originate the problem itself. At other times, the problems are thrust upon us by force of circumstance" (p. 87). Wading through the first layer of paper gave a whole new meaning to stage one of the Osborn-Parnes model; it was mess finding beyond perhaps even Osborn's imagination. The amount of money stolen was so large that the FBI was called in.

As you might expect, my aunt and uncle were highly resistant to our help. It took hours to convince them that if they did not surrender the little yellow slips to the police, a search warrant would be issued. We arrived home at 11:30 that first night in what I believe was a mild state of shock. The next day wasn't much better; we ventured back and began sorting out a mess that was, unfortunately, still growing. Two nights later, I awoke with a start at about 2:00 a.m. Sitting alone at my kitchen table I did the only thing I could—something that any student of the Master's in Creativity at Buffalo State can appreciate: I found hope in a package of Post-it Notes, a giant poster board, and a Sharpie.

What happened next is that I went into a sort of hyper-focus flow state (Csikszentmihalyi, 1990), and in a single week we accomplished the following:

- Secured financial power of attorney (I now had a whole set of friends at the bank).

- Secured healthcare power of attorney.

- Put a down payment on an assisted living home in my neighborhood.

- Froze 17 different stock accounts. Turns out my uncle (unbeknownst to any of us) was a financial genius and bought telecom stocks in the early 80's.

- Started filing five restraining orders.

- Pulled six giant Rubbermaid boxes of legal files out of the house. The police told us if we didn't do it, they would issue search warrants, as files were evidence.

- Met twice with the police department.

- Engaged our accountant to figure out my uncle's taxes. While the accountant in him documented all the "loans," he hadn't filed a tax return in six years.

- Started to clean their house, a hoarder's mess!

- Talked to two social workers and a host of other relatives.

- And, just for fun, took my dad (age 85) to the walk-in clinic because he developed bronchitis and the start of pneumonia.

While the flow state kicked in and the world dropped away, I started digging out of this mess. Sometimes without even realizing it, I was using CPS skills and tools I learned at Buffalo State. The Clustering tool suddenly became my new friend. I did several POINt (Positives, Opportunities, Issues, New thinking) evaluations with my parents. I created a giant Assisters and Resisters chart, and started to Storyboard the assisted living path, focused on the "desired stated outcome" of getting them safely in an assisted living home—which my aunt and uncle were strenuously resisting.

Thank God for Post-it Notes. They were hanging everywhere.

Creative Problem Solving Meets Design Thinking

To begin, I put every issue I could I think of, large or small, on Post-Its.[5] Initially, I was going to color-code the Post-its by issue and quickly realized it was futile; I just needed to get the ideas down. I am a big fan of group Brainstorming, but this exercise highlighted the benefits of solo Brainwriting and gave me a new appreciation for why senior-level executives tend not to participate in ideation sessions where ideas are verbally brainstormed. In some cases, the leader has to set the vision; it is not a group activity.

The next morning I began to cluster and prioritize, optimistic that a solution would emerge by lunchtime. In design thinking, Martin (2009, p. 7-9) uses the "knowledge funnel" to explain how "valuable insights" gleaned during problem exploration travel from being a seemingly-disjointed mystery to a more manageable one, and are eventually put into operation as a fixed formula (algorithm). Although using a knowledge funnel seemed like a perfectly reasonable way to sort through the Post-it Notes, it stymied me in two instances: 1) there wasn't one heuristic that would solve this problem (the issues were too complex and disjointed), and 2) my knowledge-base in dealing with the issues (ranging from Alzheimer's to financial planning) was not strong enough to create a viable algorithm (solution). In other words, the knowledge funnel component of the design thinking model could not support the challenge at hand. To be fair, the mysteries entering the funnel were highly complex and, according to Wilkinson (2006), "The more complex a situation, the harder and more time consuming it is to predict the outcome or solve a problem" (p. 53). In this crisis, we didn't have a lot of time. However, I will agree with Martin that by thinking through the disjointed aspects of the challenge, non-relevant information became background noise that didn't need be dealt with. By, as Martin (2009) calls it, "paring away extraneous information" (p. 13; e.g., the Flintstones were paying over $300 a month for basic cable and a land line because an AT&T sales person spotted an easy target) and putting it in a virtual parking lot (in the form of a giant easel sheet), I was able to show to my other family members how all issues would eventually be addressed, just not immediately.

CPS teaches us to find the desired future vision. The Clustering tool made it abundantly clear. Each main issue featured a distinct set of components, some of which needed to be immediately addressed, others extraneous. By creating the diagram below—our desired future state—I developed a sense of mental clarity: our desired future state had to focus on two issues: their finances and their health.

---

5   These issues ranged from the mundane (M needs to see a dentist) to the more serious: call police about restraining orders, call accountant to negotiate penalties with the IRS, etc. My favorite: figure out how to evict squatter (convicted felon) from their rental property in a neighborhood so bad the police warned us not to enter.

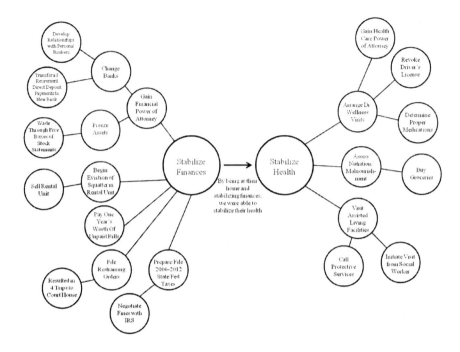

Despite the relief I felt in building a plan for moving forward, my partners in this (my parents and my sister) were unable to grasp the priorities that seemed so clear to me, which proved to be highly frustrating for all of us. In CPS terms, my late night work not only excluded them from "formulating challenges," I had failed to "explore acceptance," in particular by being insensitive to the environment—my family (Puccio et al., 2011). My family did not "own" the same level of insight I had and thus they did not internalize the plan. Csikszentmihalyi (1990) warns against this isolation, relative to the impact it might have on the leader, as well as the team:

> In a threatening situation it is natural to mobilize psychic energy, draw it inward, and use it as a defense against the threat. But this innate reaction more often than not compromises the ability to cope. It exacerbates the experience of inner turmoil, reduces the flexibility of response and, perhaps worse than anything else, it isolates a person from the rest of the world, leaving him alone with his frustrations. On the other hand, if one continues to stay in touch with what is going on, new possibilities are likely to emerge, which in turn might suggest new responses and one is less likely to be entirely cut off from the stream of life. (pp. 206-207)

Finding the True Problem

CPS is a systematic approach to solving "wicked" problems (Kolko, 2012; Martin, 2009; Reali, 2010). It is used in the production of novel and useful solutions, as defined by Puccio et al. (2011): "when we refer to change within our definition of creativity, we refer to situations in which an explicit attempt is being made to bring an idea into being that has some degree of novelty—a creative change" (p. 5). However, in large part, the value of the CPS model lies not only in systematic solution-finding, but also in situation clarification and, importantly, in finding the true problem to be solved. In a crisis situation, the time spent clarifying makes all the difference in the outcome. Family dynamics were such that everyone wanted to do something, but no one knew where to start. As a part of leading through a crisis, I needed to draw on Maxwell's (2007) law of priorities (p. 207). According to Maxwell, "successful leaders recognize that activity is not necessarily accomplishment" (p. 213), and although cleaning out the refrigerator was certainly necessary, it would not have the same impact as freezing their stocks. We needed to focus on Maxwell's three R's: what was *required,* what would give the greatest *return,* and where we would we see the greatest *reward* for our efforts (p. 216).

When examining the interconnectivity of the issues, it became overwhelmingly evident to me that the first problem to be solved involved stabilizing their financial situation. We needed to pay their back taxes and stop the penalties, and we needed money for a new furnace and roof...not to mention those mundane day-to-day needs such as food and medical care. It was also evident that in the process of solving this challenge, we would address many of the other issues the Flintstones were facing. For example, a big part of stabilizing their finances involved securing what little money they had left. In addition, spending time in their home going through the mountains of paper also meant we were with them, cleaning their home, preparing meals and essentially ensuring they were properly fed. Torrance (1979) referenced this form of solution finding as the need to find a solution that will "take into consideration the largest number of variables and will resolve the greatest number of difficulties or conflicts" (p. 58).

Ambiguity and Family Dynamics

The creativity skill of tolerance for ambiguity (Puccio et al., 2011) is easier said than done for most people. Because J and M had dementia, every conversation with them was like the movie *Groundhog Day.* My parents had a terrible time accepting this. Progress made one day was undone the next. The to-do list changed by the minute. Understanding FourSight preferences (Puccio, Miller, Thurber, & Schoen, 2012) helped. For example, my mom, a very high Clarifier, had difficulty being flexible with the to-do list. The level of frustration my dad and sister (Implementers) experienced was heartbreaking. My creative preference—Ideator—doesn't always play nicely with Clarifiers and Implementers in highly stressful situations, and as such, family battles were daily. At one family meeting I created a poster that read, "Accept that things are changing minute by minute"—another thing easier said than done.

With time, the CPS process addresses ambiguous situations. One example was the question of on-going care. My dad's first reaction to the crisis was to try to have my aunt and uncle declared incompetent by the State, an action that would result in a one-way trip to a skilled nursing facility; they would have been split up, relegated to a room with a bed and a bleak future. My first solution was assisted living, which, because we now had a handle on finances, we knew we could afford. My husband suggested we consider a home health care worker, a solution we had previously dismissed due to the perceived difficulty in finding the right person and managing him/her. Fortunately, in both divergent and convergent thinking one is instructed to be sensitive and open to novelty, so that when the answer literally came calling, we were open to it. The very day my husband suggested we revisit the home health care option, a loving neighbor called to check on J and M. In the process of chatting with her I told her we were considering assisted living. Serendipity stepped in and she replied, "*I just finished my certified nursing degree and I'm looking for a visiting nurse position.*" A window of novelty cracked open and we flew through it. Having evaluated nursing and assisted living facilities, we felt confident hiring the neighbor was a good alternative. Because we had addressed their finances, we knew we could afford to engage her.

In a loose sense, managing the caregiver of an Alzheimer's patient is very similar to rapid prototyping. On an almost daily basis we followed Martin's (2009) rapid prototyping model: we worked as a team to develop a prototype (daily goals and job description), we elicited feedback (relative to the care given and the challenges of daily care) and refined our ideas relative to what worked and didn't work, and we started all over again the next day. Reframing this new level of responsibility in the context of rapid prototyping and design thinking has helped us deal with ambiguity. Wilkinson (2006, p. 48) reports that, "We know how something should work but when we try it something else happens. This particular type of ambiguity frequently occurs when trying to predict the behavior of groups or crowds." Wilkinson (2006) believed that when a series of events happens faster than the rate at which we can discern and learn the patterns, there is a cumulative effect of the emotional impact of sudden change, causing us to be overwhelmed and to react out of fear. At the very least, we were starting to understand that constant change is the new reality. In a sense, ambiguity became the fuel driving our rapid prototyping. As Wilkinson (2006) summarized:

> In a disaster, ambiguity is high because in the first moments of a disaster, knowledge is usually very low. A good disaster manager will use the knowledge plans as a guide and start to take action to generate knowledge, being aware that things may not be as they currently think

they are and open to changing their course of action as their knowledge increases. Their decisions are based on their learning of the new world and not the rules and order of the old world, unless of course they apply (p. 122).

Tips for Employing CPS in a Crisis Situation

As I write this, the drama has mostly has subsided. Big Jimmy is sleeping soundly in jail and the white collar crimes division is pursuing a case against the nice young couple. A new furnace has been installed and paid for. Our home healthcare person is kind, loving, and terrific with J and M. Each day when we speak to them we never know what they will remember or say. It's an adventure, to say the least.

What was learned continues on. Following are guidelines for using CPS in a crisis situation, based on my experience doing just that.

Quickly identify and reinforce a desired future state

Have a vision and express it clearly in the following terms: "Our desired future state is X." The word "future" gives people hope that there *is* a future, and, importantly, a way out of the mess. Recognize not everyone will immediately grasp what you are attempting to do. This is especially important for strategic thinkers who tend to visualize situations a few steps ahead.

Communicate often and deliver messages succinctly

Frame your message with statements such as, "As we agreed...." If necessary, visually display the message and desired future state on the wall. Refer to the desired future state frequently and explain how it forms the foundation for future actions.

Collaborate when formulating challenges

Including others at the "formulating the challenges" stage is critical to buy-in. Early involvement leads to partnership and less frustration (and stronger ideas).

Visually display your strategy and supporting tactics

I created a Venn diagram depicting the situation and put the Post-It Note poster on the wall. By visually showing the challenge, we were able to work more effectively as a team.

As quickly as possible, develop an assisters/resisters matrix

Frankly, this tool held the least interest for me when I first learned about it in CRS 670: it seemed almost sophomoric. Now I believe it is tremendously powerful. You will be surprised who ends up on which side. I recommend this change to the tool's usual usage: you don't have time to convert the resisters; cut them loose. A major theme in Collins' (2001) seminal work *Good to Great*, related to how employees may need to get on or off the bus, depending on their commitment level. I have often wondered why when a new CEO comes in, a beloved employee is sometimes mercilessly dismissed. Clearly, the employee did or said something that put them on the resister side of the chart. Pick your team of assisters as swiftly as a new CEO might.

Where possible, stealthily determine the foursight profiles of your team

This will help you in communicating to them in their preferred preference. It will also allow you to delegate tasks that are most appropriate and expedite efficiency. My mom (a Clarifier) was assigned an information-gathering role. My sister (an Implementer) was instrumental in getting restraining orders filed.[6]

Do not be surprised when an assister or resistor goes rogue and attempts to take matters into their own hands

They are seeking a means of control and most likely their actions are born out of fear. However, if their actions have the potential to cause harm, make it clear why the intended action is detrimental. My dad repeatedly threatened to call the convicted felon living in my uncle's vacant rental property, *after* the police warned us not contact him.

Understand that not everyone sees your desired future state

My dad strongly opposed the idea of J and M entering assisted living. When I attempted to use the POINt evaluation tool, he told me that one of the positives associated with doing nothing was "peace of mind" for him. Be prepared for others to have a very different view of the situation.

Find humor where you can

Stuck to some loan papers (J had taken out a series of $10,000 loans that he couldn't recall doing) was a calendar from the Alzheimer's Foundation. In J's words, "it is a heck of an organization." The Flintstones were highly resistant to a home healthcare nurse. When we described it as "your neighbor Cathy is a nurse and she's going to visit you," they were delighted to have a visiting nurse.

---

6 You can take the FourSight measure yourself at foursightonline.com.

Conclusion

Clearly, what doesn't kill you makes you stronger. Understanding what the term "creative leadership" means in a real-world context is not always easy. Before this began I didn't know how to file a restraining order, or how to freeze someone's assets. Gaining financial power of attorney and subsequently managing someone's finances represented a new skill set. I had never yelled at a police officer or accused a car dealership of elder abuse. I have a whole new set of friends—detectives, home healthcare workers, caring neighbors, and even a bailiff who retrieved Big Jimmy from the county jail and wheeled him, handcuffed to a chair, into court.

Can CPS be used to navigate a crisis to a positive and successful outcome? I believe it can, assuming the groundwork has been laid and the leader has some level of exposure to the CPS process. Employing creative problem solving principles and tools can help to mitigate emotions, keep everyone moving forward and provide a framework so that the content does not become paralyzing. It is important to add a caveat: in order to be successful in a crisis situation, a creative leader must own both process and content. This is contrary to the way CPS is facilitated in traditional group settings, where a neutral facilitator manages process but stays out of the content. And yet: it's what is called for here. Leadership is not always a choice. The choice lies in how one chooses to lead—creatively or otherwise.

References

Collins, J. (2001). *Good to great: Why some companies make the leap and others don't.* New York, NY: HarperCollins.

Csikszentmihalyi, M. (1990). *Flow: The psychology of optimal experience.* New York, NY: HarperCollins.

Kolko, J. (2012). *Wicked problems: Problems worth solving. A handbook & a call to action.* Austin, TX. Austin Center for Design.

Martin, R. (2009). *The design of business: Why design thinking is the next competitive advantage.* Boston, MA: Harvard Business Press.

Maxwell, J. C. (2007). *The 21 irrefutable laws of leadership.* Nashville, TN: Thomas Nelson.

Mumford, M. D., Zaccaro, S. J., Harding, F. D., Jacobs, T. O., & Fleishman, E. A. (2000). Leadership skills for a changing world: Solving complex problems. *Leadership Quarterly, 11*(1), 11-35.

Northhouse, P. (2010). *Leadership: Theory and practice* (5th ed.). Thousand Oaks, CA: Sage Publications.

Osborn, A. F. (2001). *Applied imagination: Principles and procedures of creative problem-solving* (3rd rev. ed.). Hadley, MA: Creative Education Press. (Original work published 1953.)

Puccio, G. J., Mance, M., & Murdock, M. C. (2011). *Creative leadership: Skills that drive change* (2nd ed.). Thousand Oaks, CA: Sage Publications.

Puccio, G. J., Miller, B., Thurber, S. & Schoen, R. (2012). *FourSight presenter's guide* (3rd ed.). Evanston, IL: FourSight, Inc.

Reali, P. D. (2010). *H2 solve wicked problems*. Charlotte, NC. OmniSkills Press.

Torrance, E. P. (1979). *The search for satori and creativity*. Buffalo, NY: Creative Education Foundation.

Wilkinson, D. J. (2006). *The ambiguity advantage: What great leaders are great at*. Basingstoke, UK: Palgrave Macmillan.

BE MORE Model: A Pathway to Tap the Creative Potential of Our Children

Suzanna J. Ramos and Hector Ramos

Our children are our most precious human resource. Parents, families, and educators are in the best position to nurture the spirit of excellence in our children. They are the leaders of tomorrow. Educators and parents continually seek new ideas and methods to nurture creative children capable of making effective use of their talents and skills.

Against this backdrop, our intention is to distill fundamental insights gained from two seminal books: *Cradles of Eminence* by Victor and Mildred Goertzel (1962), and *Creating Minds* by Howard Gardner (1993). These books focus on individuals who have contributed extensively to humanity—in the arts, politics, medicine, and many others. Our belief is that every child, not just the gifted and talented, can be trained to grow up to be an adult who can meaningfully impact the lives of the people around him/her, the community or even the world.

With this belief in mind, we endeavored to find out how we can nurture our young charges to make a positive and productive impact on society.

Background

Goertzel and Goertzel's (1962) *Cradles of Eminence* is a classic example of qualitative multiple-case studies (Simonton, 1999). The authors were clinical psychologists with an interest in gifted children. The book is devoted to the family backgrounds and childhoods of 413 eminent subjects, affectionately referred by the authors as "the Four Hundred." The authors adopted a method, consisting of making generalizations about parental upbringing or childhood experiences, and then documenting each statement with numerous examples. Information about particular individuals is hardly ever detailed or extensive, and brief accounts can sometimes be misleading (Howe, 1980). However, such accounts provide fascinating insights about a person's early circumstances and childhood experiences that contribute to outstanding achievements in adulthood.

Individuals in the book include notable names such as Thomas Edison, Anton Chekhov, Charlie Chaplin, Winston Churchill, Pearl S. Buck, and Marie Curie. There are also less-common names such as Maude Adams, who were included because they met this intriguing standard: at least two books were written about them if they were born in the United States, and at least one book was written about them if they were born outside of the United States.

Gardner's (1993) *Creating Minds*, uses an approach that Simonton (1999) refers to as a comparative study that incorporates a longitudinal perspective. Gardner focuses on the commonalities in the lives and achievements of Sigmund Freud, Albert Einstein, Pablo Picasso, Igor Stravinsky, T. S. Eliot, Martha Graham, and Mahatma Gandhi. From this book, we decided to focus on their childhood experiences and family upbringing.

The following questions guided our study:

1) From these two books, what are the distinguishing childhood features that shaped these eminent individuals in their own fields and domains?

2) How can the above features be replicated so that parents have a body of knowledge to help them nurture their children to be outstanding individuals?

BE MORE Model

Using previously unpublished work by Dr. Andrei Aleinikov, we developed the BE MORE Model. This model encapsulates the various steps to help individuals accomplish more than what they can imagine. We will use this model to provide a framework from the various insights gained from the books by Goertzel and Goertzel (1962) and Gardner (1993).

Essentially, the BE MORE Model consists of the following stages:

1. B—Born

2. E—Enchanted

3. M—Mastered

4. O—Oriented

5. R—Recognized

6. E—Eternal

In the following sections, we will elaborate on each of these stages and provide examples from the two books to highlight each aspect. We also provide ideas for application by parents and teachers, including a series of questions for further reflection.

1) Born

At birth a child is a biological, physiological, and psychological entity ready for social input. It may seem trivial to include this as a stage—we are all born, after all—but this is the time when parents, primary caregivers, teachers, and mentors might be advised to assume that this new individual is on the path to becoming outstanding. These adult guides would then be driven not only by expectation but also by the belief in the future eminence of the child. They will therefore be willing to invest their time and ability to see this future come about.

Application

a) As parents, be aware, believe, and desire to consciously seek the creative potential in your children.

b) Accept compliments about your children from others. In our experience, when people compliment parents for their children's behavior, looks, etc., the response is often negative: "Oh, but they are real rascals at home," or "Well, it's just an act, they can be devils."

c) Assess your own life as potential parents and work on areas of concern so that you can strive to be good role models even before the children are born. Negative examples include too much television viewing that prevents you from being engaged in a productive hobby, dislike for reading, and lack of respect in the home. Children will be driven to imitate you as you invest your time in the learning and practice of your passions such as reading, sports, music, and others. Create a culture of learning where all the members in the family are included.

Questions for Reflection

- Are the parents (and their children) aware of the children's talents?

- How can you help them discover their talents over time?

- Do the children believe and appreciate their talents or do they doubt them?

2) Enchanted

This is the stage where the future outstanding individual is exposed to a discipline, is excited, and gets enthusiastic about it. Csikszentmihalyi (1990) refers to this discipline as the *domain*. For excitement and enthusiasm to flourish, children need to have numerous opportunities to discover their world and be able to do so in a non-threatening manner. They need to be challenged within their skill set to discover and delve deeper into new understanding and knowledge. They will therefore create their own identity as discoverers and build a unique passionate relationship with that domain. Gardner (1993) views this as the "capital of creativity" (p. 31) which they can draw from later in life. Almost all the Four Hundred in *Cradles of Eminence* (Goertzel & Goertzel, 1962) had a strong drive toward intellectual or creative accomplishment, which was present in one or both parents. Their parents were described as experimental, curious, driven, and intellectually striving. Most of all, there was a respect for learning. Curiosity and passion for learning become contagious within the family context.

Respect for learning is not the same as a love for the classroom. These parents did not push their children to perform well in school. Instead, there were strong tendencies to build directly on personal abilities, strengths, and talents, and involving their children in unusual learning situations. These situations create strong positive experiences and motivators for future desire for learning. Children will seek to replicate pleasant experiences associated with triumphs of discovery and engagement.

When Albert Einstein was four or five years old, his father showed him a compass. The young Einstein was fixated on the compass needle that did not seem to move even when he rotated the case. He was fascinated with the world of moving objects like wheels and loved to make constructions out of cards. As a result, he spent much of his time pondering scientific questions and puzzles.

The father of Robert Stephenson Smyth Baden-Powell, founder of the Boy Scouts, found time to take his children on nature hikes and encouraged them to make collections, draw, and make toys out of discarded materials. A professor in mathematics at Oxford, he had a study in his home where the children did art projects and experiments while he was on hand to provide them encouragement and advice. The children were even paid to spot errors in his articles! It was his imaginativeness and originality rather than his intellectual abilities that set the younger Baden-Powell on the road to eminence.

T. S. Eliot was enthralled by sensory impressions like smells, noises, and sights. As a result, he was drawn by candles, incense, and effigies. Since the written language was an important and dominant vehicle of communication on both sides of his family, he developed a strong capacity to capture his sensory impressions in lines of poetry. During his childhood, he cherished his experiences living along the Mississippi River and spending his summers along the shores in Massachusetts where he would read and sail. Interestingly, Einstein too had a similar period to Eliot's. This was in Italy, where he began to ponder what would happen if a ray of light were to be imprisoned. This question later proved to be fundamental to his intellectual development.

Although we have provided examples where the father seemed to be a pivotal person in the child's life, the mother was typically more driven than the father. Also, rather than the mothers being simply nurturers, they had talents, drive, and ambition to engage their children in experiential learning. Pearl S. Buck had missionary parents who brought her to China. Her mother would take her on trips to provide opportunities for her to bring comfort and assistance to people in need. This ignited in the child zeal and passion for the downtrodden where she spoke out against any injustice towards the lower echelon of society.

In *Cradles of Eminence* (Goertzel & Goertzel, 1962), it was reported that more than 90% of the Four Hundred's families showed a love for learning and achievement. Much of the source of learning and insight occurred outside the classroom—parents, public libraries, newspapers, articulate guests at the dinner table, theaters. The parents also had strong beliefs on social and religious reform movements. Children in such homes tended to emulate their parents, making it a springboard to their own outstanding achievements and providing them with plenty of opportunities to experiment with their own growing interests.

Application

a) Develop your own love for learning and intellectual pursuits so that you can be a role model of industriousness, creativity, and passion. Make discovery a great event.

b) Uncover your own values and beliefs in an issue or cause that you are passionate about and involve your children in it. These could be community service, standing up for animal rights, environmental issues, etc.

c) Engage your children by seeking their opinions of recent news or incidents, preferably at the dinner table. Ask open-ended questions to give the child an opportunity to elaborate and give details. Show appreciation for their comments by asking questions.

d) Instead of asking "What did you do in school today?", ask a question such as "What did you learn in mathematics today?" Be willing to learn from your child. Allow your children to share their discoveries.

e) Take your children on nature trails, to the zoo, and similar places, continually engaging them in conversations about what they have discovered and questions they may have.

f) View simple events in life as learning opportunities where children can ask questions, provide responses, and apply previous knowledge. For instance, at a traffic light you could ask the child, "Why are the colors red, yellow, and green? What other colors would you use?"

g) Be alert to their growing passion in a domain. It could be a discernible discipline like music or chess, but as in the case of Eliot, it may a talent that is less discernible.

h) Help your children align their beliefs to their passion or domain to help them remain motivated in their chosen discipline. Children need to believe in themselves. Help them to establish and build self-esteem, a foundation for resilience. Your children will then be able to continually learn from mistakes.

i) Teach them to journal their thoughts on their own talents and gifts.

Questions for Reflection

- How emotionally attached are the children to the development of their talents and to their vision of being an outstanding individual?

- How important is it for them?

- How much would they invest (money, time, effort, etc.) to see their talents realized?

- How can you help them create great interest and passion for their future vision of outstanding ability?

3) Mastered

This is the when the future outstanding individual has achieved a mastery level in the domain. The mastering process can take the form of formal education (in the chosen domain), mentoring, self-directed study, dedicated effort, and other practices. Gardner (1993) states that it takes at least ten years of steady and committed work at a discipline or craft before mastery can take place. Sheer hard work, constant practice, and not giving up on a certain passion are part of the mastery process.

Three out of five of the Four Hundred had serious school problems. Back then, the curriculum was rigid and much teaching was dull and uncreative. As a result, there seemed to be a rejection of the school system. Apart from perseverance and practice, what helped these eminent individuals in their childhood and early adolescence was that they were surrounded by individuals who saw a talent, interest or gift in a certain area. This greatly helped the mastery process as they had a supportive environment to hone their talents and gifts.

Sigmund Freud had a doting nurse who somehow reinforced the idea that he was a special child. Furthermore, he was surrounded by family members who recognized that he had talent and went to great lengths to organize their own routines to accommodate his needs. He had his own room with bookcases, and was not expected to dine with his family members since he had his own dining room and could pursue his studies on his own schedule.

When Albert Einstein was a young adolescent, his family regularly offered their hospitality to Max Talmey, a Russian-Jewish medical student. He gave Einstein books to read, and when he noticed that Einstein showed a keen interest in physics, Talmey gave him books dealing with topics on force and matter. This sparked a more intense desire in Einstein to doggedly pursue his passion.

When Mohandas (Mahatma) Gandhi was young, he displayed a notable interest in issues related to right and wrong. While he was playing with his friends, he gravitated towards the role of peacemaker when quarrels and fights ensued. At school, when asked to provide a false answer to a question to save his teacher from public embarrassment, he refused to do so. As a result of his talents, his parents allowed him to serve as a moral arbiter, providing him with latitude to probe family relationships and opportunities to test himself as a moral agent.

Application

a) Avoid focusing only on popular domains like sports, science, mathematics, music, art, and dance to spot talents and gifts in your children. Be sensitive to other areas like the ability to solve problems, natural leadership skills, peace-making, and unusual sensitivity to animals.

b) Apart from being mentors yourselves, identify other individuals who will be able to help hone your child's talents and gifts.

c) Allow the mentors to guide them in acquiring domain expertise and process expertise (e.g., creative and critical thinking, research strategies). Mentors can also help children develop morally, spiritually, and socially.

Questions for Reflection

- What are the areas of expertise that your children need to develop to excel in their talents?

- Who can mentor them in those areas?

- What do they need to know in order to move forward to accomplish their vision of being outstanding individuals?

4) Oriented

This is the moment when the future "beyonder" (Torrance, 1972) is oriented towards pressing social, economic, political, or environmental problems and seeks to solve those problems. In turn, this leads to high social achievement when the problem is solved, and perhaps later to the highest social award—the title of "genius." This can be seen in numerous inventions and discoveries, like X-rays, telephones, the discovery of penicillin, and pasteurization. In short, human achievements arise out of a need to address and solve the problems of a society.

Problems can be viewed as challenges to enlarge an established domain or discipline—either to push boundaries or to add value to a domain or discipline. During Freud's time, medicine and psychology were well-established disciplines with their own journals, professional organizations, and scientific methods and procedures. However, what captured Freud's interest was the analysis of dreams, unconscious processes, and one's own psyche. These were areas considered taboo by most people in the medical and psychological fields. Despite his controversial theories and research methods, he enlarged the territory of psychology, especially in the field of psychoanalysis.

Igor Stravinsky's compositional career was distinguished for its stylistic diversity. He possessed an enduring reputation as a musical revolutionary in technical innovations in rhythm and harmony, thereby pushing the boundaries of musical design. As a child, he was interested in improvisation and persevered in creating his own melodies, although his family members and teachers thought his endeavors a sheer waste of time.

Amelia Earhart and her sisters had much freedom to play and explore the neighborhood. There was a spirit of adventure, and Earhart was considered a tomboy, climbing trees and engaging in rough-and-tumble play. She expressed a desire to be the first woman to fly across the Atlantic. Although she flew with two other pilots, she was celebrated as a heroine. However, she did perform her first long solo flight and became the first woman to fly across the North American continent and back. It was unconventional for women to fly in the 1920s, but she orientated herself to be one of the few female pilots in a male-dominated domain.

Application

a) Ask your children what their big dreams are and what they hope to achieve. They may change from time to time but nevertheless, listen to their lofty ideals and never undermine them.

b) Teach your children the ability to ask crucial questions. They will be able to understand the purpose behind their learning endeavors.

c) Train them to find ways to improve things; e.g., "How might we conserve water?" or "How might we find ways to have more fun family activities?"

Questions for Reflection

- What are the "impossible" challenges they would want to solve?

- What is the type of contribution they would want to make?

- How focused are they on their subjects of interest or passion?

5) Recognized / Eternal

This is the stage when the outstanding individual is revealed, discovered, and celebrated. In the two books under study here are many familiar names: Einstein, Freud, Picasso, Churchill, Curie, and many more. They are historical figures who are considered "masters of the modern era" (Gardner, 1993, p. 6). There are also names that may not be as familiar or celebrated: Konrad Bercovci (novelist and short story writer), Kathleen Ferrier (singer), Wanda Gag (painter), and Richard Byrd (polar explorer), for example. All of these individuals are eminent people in their own right and have at least one book written about them, even if they have not become household names.

We emphasize the point that an outstanding individual is someone who makes a huge impact on the lives of people. It may be a small group like the school or workplace or it could be a city or a country. Not all of these individuals will have books written about them, but this does not diminish the impact one can have with one's creativity, talents, and gifts. Our children's achievements may not be recognized through a published biography sitting on a shelf, but they may well be recognized by the living hearts of people who are impacted and transformed by them.

Application

a) Ask children what they would like to contribute to society when they are older.

b) When your children are teenagers, get them to write a paragraph on what they would like to be remembered for.

c) Get them to share their success stories with others by giving a talk, having their own website, blogging, penning their stories in a magazine, etc.

Questions for Reflection

- How can they assess and recognize their efforts?

- Where are the sources of encouragement for them to work through their vision?

- What is their legacy?

- Who will benefit in the long run because of their accomplished vision?

Final Thoughts

Human lives have the potential to create huge legacies, great achievements, and a positive impact on society. The study of the lives of those who have achieved much can guide us on how to nurture and educate our children.

However, there can tension between our ability to envision a future and our present reality. The BE MORE model seeks to address the path between present and future. There are five elements in the BE MORE model: 1) the ability to imagine and begin a future dream, 2) to fall in love with it, 3) to master skills, 4) to become an expert of discovery in that domain, and 5) to be recognized for the accomplishment of that legacy. All of these elements possess a common factor: belief. The strongest believers are those who will pay a high price to see their dream, vision, and legacy come true. This will happen as parents, mentors, and children pay that price together. Our desire as educators is to contribute to the nurturing of those children; our fulfillment is to see their dreams come true.

References

Csikszentmihalyi, M. (1990). The domain of creativity. In M. A. Runco and R. S. Albert (Eds.). *Theories of creativity* (pp. 190-212). Newbury Park, CA: Sage.

Howe, M. J. A. (1980). *The psychology of human learning.* New York, NY: Harper and Row.

Gardner, H. (1993). *Creating minds: An anatomy of creativity seen through the lives of Freud, Einstein, Picasso, Stravinsky, Eliot, Graham, and Gandhi.* New York, NY: Basic Books.

Goertzel, V., & Goertzel, M. (1962). *Cradles of eminence.* Boston, MA: Little Brown.

Simonton, D. K. (1999). Significant samples: The psychological study of eminent individuals. *Psychological Methods, 4(4),* 425-451.

Torrance, E. P. (1972). Career patterns and peak creative achievements of creative high school students twelve years later. *Gifted Child Quarterly, 16,* 75-88.

Looking for the Big Bang in the Creation Process

João Lins

Can creativity be located as a kind of moment of inspiration at the beginning of everything that exists? What are the barriers to conceptualizing what creativity is? To better understand these questions and attempt to answer them one must take a step back in time.

In 2009, a research project for my MBA coursework required the study of a private- or public-sector company, addressing agribusiness issues. I decided to study the subject of human capital and entrepreneurship in a small rural community with approximately 1,400 inhabitants, Lajes, in the state of Pernambuco, northeastern Brazil, bringing together various aspects that made it special and different from other communities.

When the concentration of government and business investment is in urban areas, there is a stimulus for people to move from the countryside to the cities. When there is investment in the rural areas, this movement logically tends to decrease. For the study of Lajes, a fundamental question for me was to understand how people from a rural area with difficult characteristics, such as a semi-arid climate and challenging social conditions, could produce wealth, gain knowledge, generate jobs and income, and retain working class residents.

One of the things I learned, as a clue to answering this question, is that Lajes had a relatively high number of microcredit contracts, a type of bank loan brokered by the government. Nobel Peace Prize recipient Muhammad Yunus (1999) describes these loans in his book *Banker of the Poor* as credit agreements of small amounts to finance the purchase of agricultural needs (like wire for fences) or other equipment such as sewing machines. The Brazilian government authorizes these loans for people who live in the rural zone. It is also important to note that Lajes is a few kilometers away from the city of Toritama, which, despite being small, was producing 15% of all the nation's jeans. Toritama is one of the main cities of the "Clothing Industry Cluster" in the semi-arid region of the state of Pernambuco. At the time, the gross domestic product of Toritama was growing 6% per year, while the national average was 2%.

The main economic activity of Lajes was producing jeans in "informal companies," those that are not officially formed as businesses or recognized by the government. (It is estimated that this informal economy absorbs 60% of Brazil's workforce; "Brazil's informal economy," 2006). The jeans would then be sold in the city of Toritama. Encouraged by this opportunity to make their own business, the people of the community worked out of their own homes and created several small firms in the informal sector, participating in a large network of a highly creative production chain for jeans-making. The consumers of the products manufactured in this region like to wear innovative and very detailed clothes; people do not want to use simply functional clothing. Consequently, creativity is central to business survival.

During my MBA coursework, I was not very involved with the field of creativity, but through studies on entrepreneurship I had read many authors referencing the American-Austrian economist and political scientist Joseph Alois Schumpeter (1883-1950), who regarded entrepreneurship and innovation as fundamental to the development of a community, state or country. He identified the entrepreneur as a person who destroys the status quo of repetitive products, processes, and ideas and moves toward innovation (Schumpeter, 2008). It is impossible not to think about the importance of creativity in this process. It reminded me of the Big Bang theory, which leads us to reflect on a possible principle for everything. I wanted to know how the seamstresses in Lajes had created and produced the jeans, as I believed that they represented the beginning of all the jean production on that supply chain.

The 27 informal firms in the community employed approximately 270 people. With one exception, all the firms were led by women who were seamstresses formerly employed by larger companies. These firms act as semi-autonomous units because they usually have only one or two customers they call "boss." The boss is the customer who will buy the entire manufacturing output, then sell the clothes in local shops. Firms that produce jeans have limited production capacity and prefer not to accept more clients to avoid problems with quality control.

The production process in these autonomous firms has three main steps: designing the style of clothing, modeling and cutting the parts, and assembling parts for seamstresses. The designs and previously cut parts are delivered to these informal firms to be assembled. When the clothes are stitched, they then take what was produced and put other details on the clothing or sell them. See Figure 1.

While trying to understand this process of creating, some questions arose. Do the seamstresses actually create anything? Or, does following an established

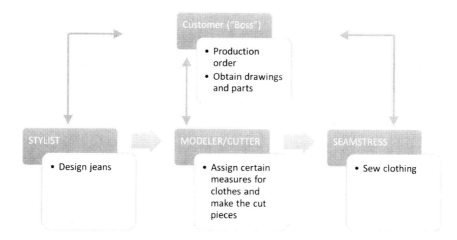

Figure 1. Simplified flow chart of the production chain

model, which cannot change, mean that there is no creativity? The notion that the seamstresses act merely as an extension of the sewing machine is inaccurate. Although the machines are programmed and also identify patterns of errors, the seamstresses, with the client, suggest modifications on the original designs. Their perceptions of the results are applied in improving the product and making it more beautiful. Despite having on hand the design that will serve as a guide for sewing, it is important for them to have a critical view of the task they are performing.

Finding Creativity in the Real World

Studying creativity will always be challenging because the subject is complex. Authors say that the word creativity stems from the Latin word *creare* ("to do"), but there are also records of a Greek word *krainen* ("hold"). This field of study also has conceptual and definitional barriers of what the phenomenon creativity means (Plucker, Beghetto, & Dow, 2004). Simply put, one can study creativity in terms of product, process, person, or press (sometimes called environment; Rhodes, 1961). It is also possible to study creativity as multifaceted, as presented by MacKinnon (1978). There are also those who invest in a kind of applied creativity based on certain techniques or processes for improving imaginative output. This seems to have originated with Osborn (1957) when he proposed the principles and procedures that came to be called Creative Problem Solving (CPS), a form of what he called "applied imagination."

I accept that creativity is a complex issue. In 2009, after completing my field research for my MBA, I did not know about the many ways of understanding creativity and that the target of my study was just that. In fact, at the time my goal was to gain understanding of the seamstresses in Lajes and the reasons for success in their business. Nevertheless, curiosity about creativity was inevitable. At that time I felt frustrated because I heard some people saying that the work of the seamstresses could not be considered creative if they followed a predetermined design.

If imagination is the basis for the creativity, then it would be reasonable that the seamstresses, who lacked the element of novelty in the construction of their pieces, nevertheless "bring life" to the jeans. This made me question the concept of being creative. Could there be a differentiation in scale between the designer and the tailor that gives the necessary qualification to be creative?

In considering the supply chain for making jeans in Lajes, should I not accept the seamstresses as people with creative actions in their production of parts for the jeans? Perhaps I should also consider the work of the modeler as less creative, as the modeler uses standard patterns of measurement to tell the designer which width and height are needed to turn a drawing into something for possible production. The modeler's job is to analyze the design prepared by the designer and transform shapes drawn on paper into standard sizes of legs and waists. After this, large pieces of jeans are stacked and cut to produce pieces of jeans.

If neither the sewers nor the modelers make a creative product, only the designer would be responsible for the creations. I know one of the designers who draws the designs of the jeans of Lajes. After each stylist completes the drawings, they are delivered to one or two modelers. The modelers determine the patterns of sizes of the pieces and cut them. The cut pieces are sent to various informal firms composed of teams of seamstresses for assembly. The supply chain is similar to the shape of a river which follows several pathways from its source (Figure 2).

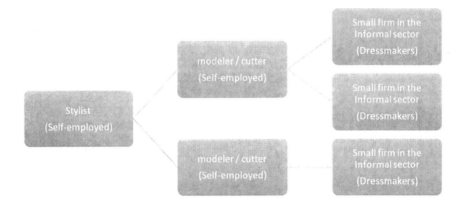

Figure 2. Simplified flow in the distribution of functions

The main problem that the designer needs to solve is to create something that is well accepted by the client, typically on a short deadline. The first step is a kind of clarifying of the situation. An observer watching a designer create a piece might think of this moment as a "big bang" moment.

The jeans proposed by the designer need to meet standards of novelty, aesthetics, functionality, and practicality for production (e.g., cost) because the designer must create designs for jeans that are viable for the client and the production owner. A pant with many pockets, for example, increases the cost of raw materials and workmanship, reducing the potential profit. Novelty that is appropriate is a creative product.

As stated by Fox & Fox (2010), creativity is a way to turn challenges into opportunities, to see new solutions to old problems, to see old problems in new ways, and to anticipate the future. The anticipation of the future is an essential element for designers. While people are buying clothes for winter, the spring models should already be ready. The designer works with a vision of the future, a key to the survival of the business cycle. Observers of innovation might not understand that a new thing is born in a unique moment. For example, as Kingdon (2012) states, innovation is fundamentally about how human beings are inspired to look in new places and how they react to the undesirable and the unexpected. Although this author has seen innovation in large companies, it is possible to observe this occurrence in enterprises of other sizes as well.

To develop an idea for a product, a conscious (or sometimes unconscious) process of creative problem solving is adopted, starting with clarifying fashion trends at that moment, understanding what themes people are valuing, and seeking information through experts of currently available products, such as fabrics and yarns. Moreover, it is necessary that the designer has a good partnership with the modeler to verify that a designer's drawing is implementable. Creativity increases when more than one individual generates ideas. Many problem solvers can be used to improve the results of the work of one designer.

Mapping CPS to Real-World Creativity

Miller, Vehar, Firestien, Thurber, and Nielsen (2011) point out that over time the CPS process has been represented by dozens of different problem-solving models. Some have six stages, some seven, some four. According to the authors, they all contribute to something good. Even Osborn proposed several models throughout his life, including the model developed in conjunction with Parnes (1967) that has persisted in various forms to this day.

Puccio, Mance, and Murdock (2011) presented a revised model of CPS (the Thinking Skills Model, or TSM) composed of three major stages: *Clarification, Transformation,* and *Implementation,* where each stage has two steps, Exploring and Formulating. The first stage, Clarification, involves *Exploring the Vision* and

Formulating Challenges; the second stage, Transformation, involves *Exploring Ideas* and *Formulating Solutions;* and the third stage, Implementation, involves *Exploring Acceptance* and *Formulating a Plan.* In addition, an executive function, *Assessing the Situation*, oversees the other stages and steps, and includes the *Gathering Data* task. Each step leads to one or more decisions. As shown in Table 1, TSM can be applied to the working process of the Lajes' stylists.

Table 1. *Creative Problem Solving process applied to Lajes jeans production*

Steps of the CPS Process	Description
Assessing the Situation	The seamstress identifies and analyzes the data, realizes what people prefer to buy according to each audience (e.g., adolescent women, children, adult men) and what competing designers are creating.
Exploring the Vision	Through participation in fairs about raw materials, research in specialized journals about fabrics, watching over storefronts in other countries, and seeking out other products that can be used, the designer explores possibilities.
Formulating Challenges	The designer analyzes the materials that meet the consumer preference. The designer also filters according to what will be accepted by the Brazilian culture.
Exploring Ideas	The designer composes drafts of proposed designs for clothing.
Formulating Solutions	The designer explores basic patterns of sizes with the modeler to complete his proposed new models of clothes.
Exploring Acceptance	The designer submits the project for acceptance to the client that requested the model of pants. The modeler and the client develop the production of the first pants.
Formulating a Plan	The project is adapted according to issues of fashion trends, production, and budget before the pants are released to the public.

Source: Adapted from Puccio, Mance, & Murdock (2011)

By comparing the processes in CPS TSM to the creative processes of a designer, it can be observed that creativity is much closer to a path with steps, in collaboration with several people, than a single "big bang" moment. Perhaps there are many "big bangs" every time. Furthermore, both small and large companies function according to the model of CPS and may benefit from the application of various tools in each step of the process. Companies like IDEO, Disney, Pixar, Google and others use various creative problem solving models but with the same concerns of the small community of designers in Lajes.

Conclusions

My observations of jean production in Toritama led to a few conclusions. First, there is no single definition to explain what creativity means. Second, a product does not emerge in a single point like the traditional Big Bang theory. Rather, creativity is a sum of steps. Third, instances of creativity can found throughout the production of a creative product, including in the seamstresses who work following a previously determined model. Finally, it is not prudent to say that the designer creates the drawings from an enlightened act. Sometimes the source of creativity is a single person, but oftentimes creativity is the result of collaboration. As shown in this essay, the universe of creativity is made fascinating by the differences and debates within this field of knowledge.

References

Brazil's informal economy absorbs 60% of workforce. (2006, July 31). Retrieved from http://en.mercopress.com/2006/07/31/brazil-s-informal-economy-absorbs-60-of-workforce

Fox, J. M., & Fox, R. L. (2010). *Exploring the nature of creativity* (3rd ed.). Dubuque, IA: Kendall-Hunt Publishing Company.

Kingdon, M. (2012). *The science of serendipity.* Chichester, UK: John Wiley & Sons.

MacKinnon, D. (1978). *In search of human effectiveness: Identifying and developing creativity.* Buffalo, NY: Creative Education Foundation.

Miller, B., Vehar J., Firestien, R., Thurber, S. & Nielsen, D. (2011). *Creativity unbound: An introduction to creative process.* Evanston, IL: FourSight.

Osborn, A. F. (1957). *Applied imagination.* New York, NY: Charles Scribner's Sons.

Parnes, S. J. (1967). *Creative behavior guidebook.* New York, NY: Charles Scribner's Sons.

Plucker, J. A., Beghetto R. A. & Dow, G. T. (2004). Why isn't creativity more important to educational psychologists? Potentials, pitfalls, and future directions in creativity research. *Educational Psychologist, 39*(2), 83-96, DOI: 10.1207/s15326985ep3902_1

Puccio, G., Mance, M., & Murdock, M. (2011). *Creative leadership: Skills that drive change* (2nd ed.). Thousand Oaks, CA: Sage.

Rhodes, M. (1961). An analysis of creativity. *Phi Delta Kappan, 4,* 305-310.

Schumpeter, J. A. (2008). *The theory of economic development: An inquiry into profits, capital, credit, interest, and the business cycle.* London, UK: Transaction Publishers.

Yunus, M. (1999). Banker to the poor: Micro-lending and the battle against world poverty. New York, NY: PublicAffairs.

Brainstorming–A Multi-Purpose Creativity Tool Past and Present

Stephen E. Gareau

The purpose of this paper is to describe how the divergent thinking tool called *brainstorming*, particularly a visual form called *mind mapping*, is being used in a graduate educational technology program as a way to help students generate ideas when designing and developing instructional multimedia products. The paper also traces possible stages in the evolution of brainstorming as we know it today.

Brainstorming–Finding Solutions to Problems and Challenges

Brainstorming might be described as a method for free, divergent thinking whereby participants generate as many ideas as possible, without applying any judgment or filters to those ideas.

As Fox and Fox (2010) pointed out, "brainstorming is the tool most closely identified with the Creative Problems Solving [CPS] process. Brainstorming was originally created by Alex Osborn in 1939 as a group technique for generating many ideas based on the divergent thinking guidelines of deferring judgment, striving for quantity...freewheeling, and building off other ideas" (p. 157).

Brainstorming comes in a range of flavors, including "stick 'em up" brainstorming (using Post-it Notes), brainwriting, blue sky brainstorming, rolestorming, negative brainstorming, and others.

New varieties of brainstorming can crop up. For instance, "brain walling" is a concept developed by Hector Ramos (H. Ramos, personal communication, June

15, 2006), whereby participants write their ideas on Post-it Notes and then place them at various discrete points along a long (preferably winding) wall. During the convergent thinking stage of problem solving (when ideas are analyzed and the best ideas selected), participants can walk along the wall to examine the ideas presented and select the best ones.

Brainstorming can use a variety of media, communication, and capture methods, including the use of text and visuals, since ideas can be expressed in a variety of ways. Brainstorming can be carried out in analog, paper-based formats, or in digital, with an increasing range of software and online tools.

As noted, brainstorming is a divergent thinking tool. Osborn, its creator, recommended that divergent thinking be separated from convergent thinking. Convergence will take place, but later. As Starko (2009) pointed out, Osborn compared the twin activities of *generating ideas* (i.e., divergent thinking) and *evaluating ideas* (i.e., convergent thinking) to driving a car, "noting that it is inefficient to drive while pushing on the gas and brake pedals simultaneously" (p. 129). Hence, there is a need to separate these two activities when engaged in the CPS process. Osborn created brainstorming as a way to generate ideas without involving any restrictive evaluation.

Possible Historical Antecedents

It is fascinating to connect brainstorming to its possible roots in human history. For instance, could it be that brainstorming goes back to man's earliest days, when our prehistoric ancestors were drawing visual and textual ideas on their cave walls? (See Figure 1.) Certainly the people of that time (as nowadays) had numerous personal and community problems to solve. We can be sure that ideas were being generated—what we can't be sure of is the context and methods by which these ideas were being generated.

Likewise, ancient Egyptians may have been engaged in an early form of brainstorming when creating hieroglyphs of logographic and alphabetic characters, written on papyrus and wood to express their ideas (see Figure 2).

Brainstorming and "Storms in the Mind"

In the world of music composition, 1841 was the "Symphony Year" for German composer Robert Schumann. It was also apparently a year for brainstorms. For instance, on Saturday evening, May 29, 1841, "Schumann noted in his personal diary that he had received inspiration in a sudden flash and was ready to write" his Symphony No. 4, which he completed in 103 days (Johnson, 2011).

Another interesting example of a version of brainstorming occurred in the mid-1960s. American music composer P. F. Sloan created the hit song "Eve of

Prehistoric petroglyphs on Newspaper Rock near Canyonlands National Park, south of Moab, Utah (Source: http://en.wikipedia.org/wiki/Petroglyph)

Prehistoric cave painting, circa. 17,000 BCE, Lascaux Caves, Lascaux, France (Source: http://fieldmuseum.org/about/multimedia/scenes-stone-age-cave-paintings-lascaux-photo-gallery)

Figure 1. Outcomes of early human ideating sessions?

Figure 2. A section of the Papyrus of Ani showing cursive hieroglyphs, circa. 3200 BC-AD 400. (Source: http://en.wikipedia.org/wiki/File:Papyrus_Ani_curs_hiero.jpg)

Destruction" in the early morning hours between midnight and dawn in mid-1964. He was only 19 years of age at the time. The song was one of five that he wrote that evening—three of which became notable.

According to Sloan (1999), the most outstanding experience he had in writing this song was a kind of inner brainstorm,

> hearing an inner voice inside of myself for only the second time. It seemed to have information no one else could've had. For example, I was writing down this line "think of all the hate there is in Red Russia." This inner voice said "No, no it's Red China!" I began to argue and wrestle with that until near exhaustion. I thought Red Russia was the most outstanding enemy to freedom in the world, but this inner voice said the Soviet Union will fall before the end of the century and Red China will endure in crimes against humanity well into the new century! (p. 1)

The line in the song eventually read: "Think of all the hate there is in Red China, then take a look around to Selma Alabama..." According to Sloan (1999), "this inner voice is inside of each and every one of us, but is drowned out by the roar of our minds!" (p. 1). Singer Barry McGuire recorded the song, and it went on to become *Billboard* magazine's number one song for a week in late September 1965.

Brainstorming and the Stream of Consciousness

A concept related to brainstorming and developed in 1890 by American philosopher and psychologist William James is *stream of consciousness*. As a way to help people understand their mental processes, James (1890/1950) described *stream of consciousness* as the continuous and contiguous flow of thoughts, feelings, sensations, images, impressions, and memories—all unfiltered and uncensored. As James explained, "consciousness does not appear to itself chopped up in bits… it flows. A 'river' or 'stream' are the metaphors by which [consciousness] is most naturally described" (p. 239). When stream of consciousness is applied to the writing of ideas, it is typically characterized by a lack of "correct" punctuation or syntax, favoring a looser, more incomplete style. Interestingly, this is also typically how ideas are generated and recorded during a brainstorming session: using a loose, open, freewheeling, and incomplete style.

A possible outcome of a brainstorming session is a *mind map* or a *concept map*. A *mind map* is a diagram used to represent words, ideas, tasks, or other items linked to a central key word or idea (Buzan & Buzan, 1996). In contrast, a *concept map* is a diagram showing ideas or concepts as well as the relationships among those ideas or concepts. Whereas mind maps are based on radial hierarchies or tree structures around a single, central idea, concept maps are less structured, and are based on connections between ideas and concepts in more diverse patterns. Since multiple hubs or clusters can be created, concept maps are more free form, unlike mind maps which fix on a single central idea. What is particularly useful about both mind maps and concept maps is that they can help us to visualize (at a single glance) the big picture of what it is we are trying to understand and/or create.

Mind maps and concept maps are closely related to other similar types of brainstorming tools such as topic maps, spidergrams, spidergraphs, spider diagrams (used in mathematics and logic), and others. Mind maps and concept maps can be hand-drawn on paper. They can also be created in digital format using an increasing range of available software.

Application of Brainstorming in the Classroom: The Design of Instructional Multimedia Products

SUNY Buffalo State has an educational technology graduate program. The main audience of the program is K-12 teachers from a wide variety of curriculum areas. A main goal of the program is to help teachers learn how to design and develop instructional materials for use in their own classrooms. There is instruction on how to use a variety of media, design principles and tools, and development tools. A main design process is the ADDIE model of instructional design, which is used in a number of courses in the program, including Instructional Technologies (EDC 601), Authoring for Educators (EDC 604), and Master's Project (EDC

690). In these courses, students are asked to create instructional products using a range of media, including text, graphics, photographs, video, audio, animation, hardware, software, etc. The ADDIE model is a common design process that includes five stages: Analysis, Design, Development, Implementation, and Evaluation. Each stage typically includes a series of steps, and there is often iteration within and between stages.

In designing and developing instructional multimedia products, students are asked to brainstorm project ideas during the following steps of the Analysis stage:

1. Identify current instructional problems/challenges. Brainstorm classroom challenges/needs (and create an associated concept map) using wish-statement starters such as: "Wouldn't It Be Great If...", and "I Wish...."

2. Select one of these challenges/needs to address. Identify the subject area that is associated with this challenge/need.

3. After identifying the subject area, brainstorm potential topics to include in the design and development of an instructional product that could help to meet the challenge/need selected. Create a mind map of potential topics, and show links (relationships) between topics.

Conclusion

Brainstorming, i.e. the "storming of minds" for new and novel insights and ideas, is an invaluable thinking and problem solving tool that has long served humankind in a multitude of ways and will, no doubt, continue to do so in the future. As with almost any collection of tools, the only limits to such thinking tools are the mental limits of their users as to where, when, and how they might be applied. No tool is perfect for every problem, yet brainstorming seems to be one of those versatile "all-purpose multi-tools" that can play a role in the solution of almost any problem.

References

Buzan, T., & Buzan, B. (1996). *The mind map book: How to use radiant thinking to maximize your brain's untapped potential.* New York, NY: Plume.

Fox, J. M. & Fox, R. L. (2010). *Exploring the nature of creativity* (3rd ed.). Dubuque, IA: Kendall Hunt Publishing Company.

James, W. (1950). *The Principles of Psychology* (rev. ed.). New York, NY: Dover Publications, Inc. (Original work published 1890.)

Johnson, J. (2011, September 14). Program Notes, October 2011. Retrieved from http://soniclabyrinth.blogspot.com/2011/09/program-notes-october-2011.html

Sloan, P. F. (1999). *P. F. Sloan: In his own words—the stories behind the songs.* Retrieved from http://www2.gol.com/users/davidr/sloan/aboutsongs.html

Starko, A. J. (2009). *Creativity in the classroom: Schools of curious delight* (4th ed.). New York, NY: Routledge.

Three C's: Exploring a Continuum of Creativity

Pamela A. Szalay

There is a need for a developmental model of creativity: a growth model that bridges the gap between the two extremes often suggested by the word creativity. On one extreme there is the type of creativity we imagine occurs in preschools. On the other, there is the eminent creativity that occurs at places like Apple.

The "preschool" kind of creativity is one in which all self-expression is praised. There is no need to conform and no fear of judgment. Young or old, this is the level of creativity where beginners can try a new skill and be rewarded. It's what I refer to as creative self-expression and it is an important first step in learning and being creative. The eminent level of creativity is miles away from this. It's expertise and novelty married to sophisticated execution. It's Steve Jobs unveiling the first Apple computer, the iPod and the iPhone. It's Picasso's cubism. It's the cure for cancer.

Society tends to understand creativity as A or B. It seems to be something we look down on, or up to. It's either the stuff of kids, or the output of geniuses. Yet there must be something in between. Is it possible to develop a comprehensive model that reveals a continuum of creativity, with key developmental milestones, that would help us better navigate the way from emergent creative outpourings to finely-tuned creative maturity?

At this point, it is helpful to address another dichotomy: that of "little-c" and "big-C" creativity (Simonton, 2010). This model, also, suggests two views of creativity and has an undefined middle ground. Essentially, little-c creativity conveys the idea that all of us can engage in "everyday creativity" and problem solving. We can come up with novel ways of overcoming problems that make us happy, save us money, entertain our friends, and help us get our work done. In contrast, big-C creativity refers to the type of creativity that leaves an enduring mark on society, perhaps through the invention of a product or the sharing of an idea that changes how people live, work, or think.

When the model of little- and big-C creativity is mingled with the notion of a creativity continuum ranging from creative expression to creative maturity, creative expression seems to have a stage of development that precedes little-c creativity. One response is to label this early stage as "beginning-c" creativity, a stage marked by high levels of imagination and exploratory play. Then little-c creativity would be a middle stage and there would be, for now, three stages of creative maturity: beginning-c, little- or middle-c, and big- or mature-C.

Exploring these ideas further is important to improving the assessment and nurture of creativity, whether in the home, in schools or in the workplace. Table 1 displays a suggestion for approaching the challenge of defining the developmental stages of creativity within an individual. I do not offer it as a finished model but as fuel for a larger conversation about how creativity can be applied and play a greater, more active role in education, childhood development, learning and instruction, talent development and beyond.

References

Simonton, D. K. (2010). Creativity in highly creative individuals. In J. C. Kaufman & R. J. Sternberg (Eds.), *The Cambridge handbook of creativity* (pp. 174-188). Cambridge, UK: Cambridge University Press.

Table 1: *Three C's: A model for exploring a continuum of creative development*

Stage	Beginning-c	Little-c (or Middle-c)	Big-C (or Mature-C)
Characteristics	Self–Expression	Deliberation	High Performance
	Constraints are low and/or developmentally appropriate. Individuals are learning to experiment and express self (ideas, actions, emotions).	Constraints are a reality. Individuals address challenges with purpose and are responsive to feedback/evaluation.	Constraints are complex and demanding. Individuals are self-evaluative, contextually aware, and able to balance competing demands.
Environment/ Context	Low Risk	Medium Risk	High Risk
	The environment is marked by safety: a small non-threatening audience, with little or no repercussions for being "wrong."	This could be called a stretch opportunity. The audience is larger and more demanding. There might be negative consequences if solutions fail.	This is creativity in a highly visible or public arena. If ideas/products fail, serious negative consequences may affect the individual as well others (entire organizations or societal groups).
Focus/ Challenge	Education of Self	Everyday Problem Solving	Problem Solving for Innovation
	Learning about known facts through discovery learning; building a personal schema; problem solving that is novel to the individual, but not to society.	Learning to solve problems that are increasingly complex, ambiguous and unique. Known solutions and/or methodologies might be selected and applied.	Alone or as part of a group, the individual solves complex, ambiguous, and unique problems for which there are no existing models or methodologies to apply.
Knowledge Area Mastery	Ignorance/Novice	Competence	Mastery
	Individual may have no expertise in any domain.	Competence, skill and/or experience in at least one domain is important.	Mastery and expertise in at least one domain is needed, supplemented by competence and skills in other domains.
Lifestyle/ Motivation	Play	Emerging Discipline	Work-Play Balance
	Intrinsic motivation, play and curiosity drive the individual's action. Reward is connected to the pleasure of the task itself, or a very-immediate positive consequence. This stage is characterized strongly by being "in the moment."	Play is still important, but extrinsic factors may now play a role in pushing the individual into challenging situations. Discipline deepens as the individual begins to appreciate future payoffs and becomes willing to endure unpleasant tasks in the "now."	To flourish creatively, the individual achieves a balance between play and discipline, fun and work. Factors in the individual's work and personal life sustain a good balance of intrinsic and extrinsic motivating factors. Individual may have worked to secure those factors.
Outcome/ Influence	Outcome is mostly meaningful to the individual	Outcome is meaningful to a group	Outcome is meaningful to a large community or to all of society

About the Contributors

Alison L. Murphy is a partner at Murphy Marketing Research/TrendTown. She specializes in new products and creativity training.

Alison@murphymarketing.com
www.murphymarketing.com

Amy Frazier is a consultant, facilitator and trainer in Seattle, WA. She offers creativity, team building and leadership programs through her company Stages of Presence.

amyefrazier@gmail.com
www.stagesofpresence.com | Twitter: @aefrazier

Catherine Tillman is a writer and creativity coach.

tillmancatherine@gmail.com
www.catherinetillman.com | Twitter: @cattillman

David Hoffman teaches high school English and is actively pursuing educational reform.

HoffmansASH@gmail.com
www.linkedin.com/in/innovateeducation | Twitter: @TheParticleSon

Dixie Hudson is a professor in interior design at the British Columbia Institute of Technology in Vancouver, Canada.

Dixie_Hudson@bcit.ca

Doug Stevenson is a creativity facilitator and trainer living in the Chicago area.

doug.goodideas@gmail.com
Twitter: @MadCreative

Hector Ramos holds a Ph.D. in Educational Psychology (Creativity) from Texas A&M University, where he teaches creative thinking as an assistant lecturer.

hreina@gmail.com

Jeff Olma is an instructor of creativity and English at Florida State College at Jacksonville.

j_olma@comcast.net

Jeffrey Glaub is a music educator in the Buffalo Public Schools System.

jeffrey.glaub@gmail.com

João Lins is a college professor at State University of Pernambuco – Brazil.

joao_lins@hotmail.com

John Yeo is a consultant on curriculum innovations at the National Institute of Education, Nanyang Technological University, Singapore.

yeojohn75@gmail.com

Josh Mahaney is an innovation catalyst for the NBA's Orlando Magic.

josh.j.mahaney@gmail.com
www.linkedin.com/in/joshmahaney

Julia Roberts helps writers understand their own creativity—often for the first time in their lives—so they can write better and steer the course of their creative career powerfully.

julia@decodingcreativity.com
decodingcreativity.com | Twitter: @juliadecodes

Maisha Drayton is a deputy director with CAI, Inc. a capacity building organization based in New York City.

maisha.drayton@gmail.com
www.linkedin.com/in/maisha-drayton-ms-071b7926 | Twitter: @maisha_D

Maria Macik is a curriculum consultant at Texas A&M University, and a novelist.

mlazo@tamu.edu
https://sites.google.com/site/lazomaria09

Marta Ockuly teaches creative process at Eckerd College, lectures internationally about reimagining creativity and making peace with art.

magicalmarta@aol.com

www.joyofquotes.com | Twitter: @quotejoy

Maureen Vitali is the director of organizational effectiveness for a technology and services startup in Houston, TX.

maureenvitali5@gmail.com

Pamela Szalay is an educator and consultant promoting creativity and compassion for all. She is the Director of Programs at the Beyonder Academy and President of Imagine & in Buffalo, NY.

szalay.pamela@gmail.com

www.beyonderacademy.com | Twitter: @musingbypam

Randah Taher likes to play in sandboxes with toys such as: design leadership, social innovation, creative environments facilitation, and visual and participatory design methodologies.

ttrtaher@hotmail.com

http://contagiouscreativity.wordpress.com | Twitter: @randahtaher

Robin Lee Harris recently retired from a fruitful career in higher education. She is now working on developing her creative scientific inquiry web presence.

harrisrl@buffalostate.edu

www.battandrobin.com

Russell Schneck works with organizations of all sizes respond to the opportunities and challenges of change and complexity by applying critical thinking, creative thinking, and systems thinking principles, tools, and methods to develop and support individual and group problem-solving capabilities.

russell.schneck@gmail.com

Ryan Irish lives in Buffalo, NY.

iwish311@aol.com

Sandra A. Budmark is director of organizational development for Wendel, an architectural and engineering design firm in Buffalo, NY.

sbudmark@wendelcompanies.com

Shane Sasnow is a change management consultant with expertise in strategy and innovation.

avshane@hotmail.com

https://www.linkedin.com/in/shanesasnow

Stephen E. Gareau is a professor of learning design and technology at SUNY Buffalo State.

sgareauca@yahoo.com

http://cis.buffalostate.edu/faculty/stephen-e-gareau

Steven Martin is the founder of Business Solutions – The Positive Way, a business consulting firm, and is an active volunteer with SCORE.org.

smartin@profitpro.us

www.profitpro.us

Suzanna Ramos graduated with a Ph.D. in Educational Psychology from Texas A&M University. She is an assistant lecturer and teaches courses on educational psychology and child development for educators.

suzannaramos@gmail.com

Tiana N. Thompson is direct support professional for New York Civil Service. She is the author of *Visually Paired Through Creativity*.

t.tiana52@yahoo.com

www.linkedin.com/in/tiana-thompson-418a0b99 | Twitter: @Visuallycr8tive

Troy Schubert is a category innovation engineer, men's and women's training, at Nike.

https://www.linkedin.com/in/troy-schubert-8503a44

About the Editors

Jon Michael Fox is the senior lecturer at the International Center for Studies in Creativity at SUNY Buffalo State. Additionally, Mike consults as a trainer and facilitator in creativity and innovation development. He designs and delivers workshops in creativity and innovation for the public sector, inventors, designers, educators, and the business community across the globe.

Mike is qualified in the Myers-Briggs Type Indicator, Emotional Intelligence, FourSight, and Appreciative Inquiry. His book, *Exploring the Nature of Creativity* (3rd edition) examines the multi-faceted nature of creativity and how to nurture it.

Mike's background is diverse. He has been an executive, a landscape architect, prairie restoration consultant, author, and airline pilot. In his spare time, Mike does museum-quality restorations of antique aircraft.

Mike is a member of Alpha Zeta professional agriculture fraternity, the Airplane Owners and Pilots Association, and the Experimental Aircraft Association. He holds a Bachelor of Landscape Architecture degree from the University of Minnesota and a Master of Science degree in Creativity from Buffalo State.

Contact:
Jon Michael Fox
International Center for Studies in Creativity
SUNY Buffalo State, 1300 Elmwood Avenue, Chase Hall 244
Buffalo, New York 14222-1095
(716) 878-6214
foxjm@buffalostate.edu

Ronni Lea Fox is a professional writer, former teacher, actress, and chef. She has conducted classes and workshops on creative writing, including character and plot development, publishing and editing, journaling, group writing activities, and playwriting.

Ronni's work has been featured in numerous magazines. She wrote a successful radio play that was featured on a number of radio programs including National Public Radio. She designed a commercial for the National Cancer Society that enjoyed a three-year run.

Ronni's most recent literary efforts have been co-authoring *Exploring the Nature of Creativity* and developing her Hat Tricks workshop, which she recently conducted for the National Association of Gifted Children, and Colegio Panamericano in Colombia, South America.

Contact: ronnifox@hotmail.com

About
the International Center
for Studies in Creativity

The International Center for Studies in Creativity (ICSC) is known around the world for its personally transformative undergraduate, graduate and distance programs that cultivate skills in creative thinking, innovative leadership practices and problem solving skills.

ICSC is the first program in the world to teach the science of creativity at a graduate level: Our Graduate Certificate program includes six courses that focus on creative process, facilitation, assessment, training, theory and leadership. With an additional four courses, including a master's project or thesis, students can complete a Master of Science degree in creativity and change leadership. Graduate students can pursue their degree on campus or via the "Distance Program," which offers a blend of on-campus and virtual classrooms.

For nearly 50 years, ICSC is proud to have contributed to seminal research to the field of creativity. ICSC is part of Buffalo State, State University of New York.

To learn more, please visit creativity.buffalostate.edu.

ICSC Press

Created in 2012, ICSC Press is the imprint of the International Center for Studies in Creativity. The mission of the press supports the vision of the Center to ignite creativity around the world, facilitating the recognition of creative thinking as an essential life skill.

ICSC Press's goal is to put the work of our best teachers, thinkers, and practitioners into the hands of a wide audience, making titles available quickly and in multiple formats, both paper and electronic. Our titles include:

- *Creativity Rising: Creative Thinking and Creative Problem Solving the in 21st Century,* by Gerard J. Puccio, Marie Mance, Laura Barbero Switalski, & Paul D. Reali

- *Big Questions in Creativity 2013,* Cynthia Burnett & Paul D. Reali, Eds.

- *Big Questions in Creativity 2014,* Mary Kay Culpepper & Cynthia Burnett, Eds.

- *Big Questions in Creativity 2015,* Mary Kay Culpepper & Cynthia Burnett, Eds.

- *Big Questions in Creativity 2016,* Paul D. Reali & Cynthia Burnett, Eds.

- *My Sandwich is a Spaceship,* by Cyndi Burnett & Michaelene Dawson-Globus

- *Business Creativity and the Creative Economy* (journal), ed. by Mark A. Runco

- *Journal of Genius and Eminence,* ed. by Mark A. Runco

To learn more, to purchase titles, or to submit a proposal, visit icscpress.com.